Contents

Fethullah Gulen

The Gulen movement is attracting increasing and sometimes hostile attention both inside Turkey and beyond as a result of its increasing activity, wealth, and influence. Inspired by the thoughts of its founder, Sufi scholar Fethullah Gulen, it has established hundreds of educational institutions, as well as media outlets, dialogue platforms, and charities. Well-established in Turkey, it has expanded into the wider Turkic world and, increasingly, beyond. Yet its structure, ambitions, and size remain opaque, making assessment of its impact and power difficult.

Introduction

Recent developments have led to an upsurge of curiosity about the Turkish Sufi scholar Fethullah Gulen and his legion of followers, known as Fethullahci, both in his native country and abroad. One factor contributing to this attention was Gulen's summer 2008 election as the world's leading intellectual in a poll organized jointly by the British Prospect magazine and the U.S. publication Foreign Policy, in which over half a million votes were registered for a candidate who had hitherto been unknown to Prospect's editor.

Prospect's analysis of the poll highlighted how relatively high levels of Turkish internet use generated a specifically Turkish effect in such polls. Prospect also identified in Gulen's victory the emergence of a new kind of intellectual, "*one whose influence is expressed through a personal network, aided by the internet, rather than publications or institutions.*"

These observations offer a penetrating insight into the mechanisms of Gulen's influence and the nature of the Gulen movement. Prospect additionally noted how votes for Gulen mounted in the wake of publicity for the poll in the Gulen-inspired Turkish newspaper

Zaman and a host of other Gulen websites. This testified to the legendary "*efficiency and discipline*" and "*organizational ability*" of the Fethullahci.

There is a hint of something sinister in this interpretation of Gulen's victory, implying as it does central direction rather than spontaneity. Secular Turks share such suspicions, and conspiracy theories abound in Turkey concerning both the source and level of the movement's funding and the nature of its ultimate ambitions.

Indeed, both are obscure. It is often alleged that the Gulen movement receives funding, either alternatively or simultaneously, from the CIA, Saudi Arabia, Iran, and the Turkish state.

Gulen himself has lived in somewhat hermit-like exile in Pennsylvania since 1998, ostensibly due to ill-health but also as a consequence of fears for his freedom should he return to Turkey. He was charged in 1999 for "*establishing an illegal organization in order to change the secular structure of the state and to establish a state based on religious rules.*"

Although he was acquitted in 2006, the judgment was appealed, and it was not until June 2008 that the acquittal was finally upheld, thus clearing the way for his safe return to Turkey. In the West, most would probably concur with The Economist, which has noted the generally good reception received there by the Gulen movement, whose security services "*have not detected any hidden ties with extremism.*"

On the other hand, according to the American "neo-conservative" Michael Rubin, if Gulen does return to Turkey "*Istanbul 2008 may very well look like Tehran 1979.*" Rubin anticipates millions turning out to greet Gulen on his return to Turkey, his issuing of fatwas (religious edicts) designed to distance Turkey from its official secularism, the restoration of the caliphate, and the subversion of the rule of law "*to an imam's conception of God.*"

In more measured fashion, Hakan Yavuz, a U.S.-based Turkish scholar of Islam in Turkey, has been quoted as asserting that the Gulen movement is "*the most powerful movement right now in the country.... The point where they are today scares me. There is no other movement to balance them in society.*"

The movement's activities abroad sometimes arouse comparable suspicions. The Russian authorities, fearful of any indications of Islamic or pan-Turkic revivalism within their borders, have recently tried to close down a Gulen school in St. Petersburg as part of a wider campaign against the movement's activities and influences, a campaign which has included bans on the works of the Sufi teacher Said Nursi, from whom Gulen draws much of his inspiration.

In light of all this, it is interesting to note that the U.S. authorities chose to reject Gulen's application for the right of permanent residence in the United States on the grounds of his insufficient renown, a decision ruled improper by a federal judge in July 2008.

Clearly Gulen and the Fethullahci are divisive, but they have also been described by The Economist as "*one of the most powerful and best-connected of the networks that are competing to influence Muslims round the globe.*" In addition to its global activism, the movement constitutes a major part of Turkey's current social and political evolution, signified by the electoral fortunes of the ruling Justice and Development Party (Adalet ve Kalkinma Partisi, AKP), with which it overlaps.

Gulen's Thinking

One cannot understand the nature of the movement without some mention of Fethullah Gulen's thinking. Although this has evolved towards more universalistic, pluralistic, liberal, and democratic values, in large measure it remains rooted in Turkey's particular circumstances and experiences. For Gulen, Kemalist Turkey's "top-down" imposition of a dogmatic secularism has distanced swathes of Turkish society from the governing elite. Gulen prefers to draw inspiration from the Ottoman model of state-society relationships. Although the empire's rulers were guided by their faith, the Ottoman system of governance was not theocratic.

Public laws were formulated on the basis of the state's needs rather than in accordance with Islamic law (Shari'a). For Gulen, the state has a functionally secular responsibility to provide internal and external security and stability for its citizens. Gulen's state-centrism even led him to sympathize with Turkey's 1980 military coup, regarding it as appropriate that the state protect itself and its citizens against the chaos that was threatening to engulf Turkish society.

Thus, Gulen is not in favor of the political implementation of Shari'a, though the freedom to express one's faith should be respected. He is opposed to "political Islam," and even sympathized with Turkey's 1997 "post-modern coup" that removed Necmettin Erbakan's Welfare Party from power, although Gulen was himself caught up in the crackdown on religious activity that came in its wake. He believed that Erbakan and his followers were embarked on the first steps towards an "Iranianization" of Turkish political and social life.

Gulen believes that there is no necessary contradiction between Islam and modernity. Indeed, Turkish Islam's more adaptable and less doctrinal Sufi traditions have enabled Turkey, with its democratization, free market economy, and secular political system, to incorporate aspects of modernity barely found elsewhere in the Muslim world.

A key to his thinking is that Islam should positively embrace science, reason, democratization, and tolerance. It should not shield itself from other faiths, other ideas, or from scientific and technological progress. Gulen believes that the relative (to the West) economic and moral poverty of so much of the Islamic world is explained by its attachment to misplaced and dogmatic interpretations of Islam, not Islam per se.

Indeed, he believes Turkey can lead the Islamic world toward this realization, and for all his proclaimed universalism there is also a pronounced "Turkish-ness" to his thinking. Turkish society is nationalistic, and some of this flavor has been absorbed by Gulen and the Fethullahci.

For Gulen, the key to Islam's adaptation to the modern world does not lie in direct political activity and organization. Rather, Gulen propagates a kind of "educational Islamism" as opposed to a "political Islamism."

Thus, educational curricula should emphasize science, technology, and instruction in the English language. In place of faith teaching Gulen advocates the cultivation of spiritual, moral, and behavioral values, of tolerance, respect, openness, and the like. Indeed, Gulen feels that the West has forsaken the spiritual dimension of human existence.

Through the internalized spiritual transformation of individuals, a wider social transformation will evolve and, indirectly, a (re-) "Islamized" version of modernity. Thus, politics should be "Islamized" only via a bottom-up process and indirectly, in which people and state are reconnected through a shared attachment to and internalization of values.

It is an approach that resembles a kind of "long march through the institutions." In this sense, Gulen's mission can be said to be a political project, but one that aspires to achieve its goals indirectly. People of faith as well as learning, a "Golden Generation," should be cultivated and encouraged to dedicate their lives to the service (hizmet) of the people and to inspire them towards the movement's objectives.

The emphasis on spirituality in Gulen's thinking is partly explained by his attachment to Turkey's "folk Islam," Sufism. Specifically, Gulen derives inspiration from the writings of the prominent Kurdish religious authority Said Nursi (1877-1961).

His Nur (Light) movement was similarly distinguished by its advocacy of reason, progress, and tolerance, and its quietism towards direct political involvement. Even if Turkish Islam's uniqueness is sometimes exaggerated, there is little doubt that its sects, saints, and eclecticism can be offensive to other Muslims, as can its "moderation."

Sufism also typically features the kind of master-disciple relationships replicated today by the inspiration Gulen provides his followers. Widespread membership of Sufi sects has long persisted in secular Turkey, generally concealed from the country's suspicious rulers.

Gulen has also advocated both local and global interfaith and inter-civilizational dialogue, and to this end met with Pope John Paul II in Rome in 1998, and inside Turkey with Patriarch Bartholomeos, head of the Greek Orthodox Fener Patriarchate in Istanbul, the former Chief Rabbi of Turkey's Jewish community David Aseo, as well as with numerous other high-profile Jewish and Christian figures.

In its support for and sponsorship of such activities, the Gulen movement seeks both to counter the impact of the more violent fundamentalist strains in modern Islam - Gulen has repeatedly condemned terrorism as "un-Islamic"- and to undermine wherever it can Huntington's "Clash of Civilizations" thesis.

Gulen's championing of interfaith dialogue springs in part from his recognition of the shared theological origins of Islam, Christianity, and Judaism- although in his appeal for interfaith dialogue and tolerance Gulen incorporates Buddhism and Hinduism too- and Muhammad's injunction to respect the "people of the book." The transcendental quality of faith is for Gulen a unifying force that outweighs theological differences.

His commitment to dialogue with the Judeo-Christian world is also related to his admiration for Western modernity, liberalism, and technological and economic prowess. Gulen's frequent and approving references to the "Global Village" express his perception that the phenomena of globalization have so bound together the fates of peoples that conflict between them serves nobody's interests.

Characteristically, he again draws upon the multi-faith and multicultural example of the Ottoman Empire, which he adduces as evidence of the capacity of diverse peoples to live together harmoniously. The flavor of Gulen's thinking is then distinctly moderate, and offers little credence to some of the wilder accusations against him.

The Fethullahci

In the wake of Gulen's appointment as a state-employed religious preacher to Izmir in 1966, a loose network of students, teachers, professionals, businessmen, and the like began to gather around him and to coalesce as a spontaneous "social movement" inspired by Gulen's example.

Its first venture into the wider propagation of its philosophy came in the form of summer schools, from which it progressed to the establishment of teaching centers (dershane), often dormitories, to prepare religious students for university admission. These remain an important element in the inculcation of Gulen's values, not least through a "mentoring" system found throughout the movement's educational establishments and its wider "structure."

The dershane are also a prime source of recruits. As it blossomed, so it attracted the attention of Turkey's secularist state establishment. Gulen himself served a seven-month spell in prison in the early 1970s for propagating religion, and again attracted uncomfortable attention both during the 1980s and, as already noted, in the late 1990s.

The network did not openly blossom as a major educational, social, and religious movement until the early 1980s, when in the wake of the military coup of 1980 the space for religious activity was expanded, a policy inspired by the so-called "Turkish-Islamic synthesis." This advocated a fusion between Turkish national identity and the Islamic faith, in the hope that a (state- managed) religiosity would offer a politically less threatening antidote to the leftism that had contributed to the social chaos of the preceding decade.

It has been argued that "*the rural and pious masses of Anatolia remained largely unaffected by the cultural re-engineering*" of Kemalism, and that Turkey has remained a "torn" society a la Huntington. The wider "democratization" and opening up of social, economic, and political life in Turkey after 1983 reinforced this "center-periphery" encapsulation of Turkish politics and society.

Turkey's increased pluralism has enabled its more devout and conservative provincial hinterland to challenge the Kemalist, secular, "Westernizing" and urban center. This ideological rift has been reinforced by the ascendance of a more traditional, pious Anatolian business and professional class.

The Gulen movement also profited from this post-1980 liberalization, which created a space for its media, educational, and financial activities free from the control of the statist secular establishment and which was accompanied by, and contributed to, a more general "Islamization" of Turkish public life.

Turkey's "new" class of businessmen, professionals, teachers, and intellectuals form the core of the Fethullahci. This middle class profile is not quite coincident with the newly-urbanized working class or the rural poor who provide the backbone of the AKP's electoral support.

Gulen followers range from extremely pious individuals - often teachers and preachers and those engaged in the movement's dialogue activities, who are inspired by the Islamic principle of hizmet, and whose lives are dedicated to the propagation of the values and ideas of Fethullah Gulen - to the more occasional and more pragmatic sympathizers, such as businessmen, politicians, journalists, and increasingly even officials of the supposedly secular Kemalist state.

Collectively, these might be regarded as Gulen's "Golden Generation." The movement's pious activists are inclined towards constant and somewhat uncritical reference to Gulen's writings. Such "true believers" can convey the impression of "cultism," and can perhaps be likened to early Christian sects, certainly in their motivation but perhaps also in their spontaneity.

There seems little reason to doubt the debt of the movement's business backers to Gulen's philosophy, the sincerity of their Islamic approach to their wider social and moral obligations, their desire to please God, and their voluntarism. Zakat is one of the five pillars of

Islam, and obliges Muslims to donate 2.5 percent of their wealth to worthy causes. Sadaqa, or voluntary charity, can inspire the wealthy to donate in excess of this minimum.

Many rich Gulen sympathizers do indeed donate a large percentage of their personal wealth, as expressions of their commitment. Businessmen, typically forming tightly-knit circles drawn from a particular town or locality and whose relationships rely heavily on mutual trust, donate - in money or in kind - to the building of schools and the like as acts of Islamic charity. Such "giving" might also bring a commercial return in the form of contracts or "profits" from a venture's revenue-raising capacity, although the general principle is that ventures should be self-financing and that any surplus funds be ploughed back.

Initially benefitting from some protective cover from Prime Minister Turgut Ozal, reckoned to be a sympathizer, the movement has since gone on to open around 200 schools in Turkey since its first was established in 1982, universities such as Fatih in Istanbul, hospitals, charities, a television channel (Samanyolu TV) - which now has plans to broadcast to the Turkish community in Germany - a radio station (Burc FM), a mass-circulation daily newspaper (Zaman) - which in addition to its online English-language edition also publishes elsewhere in the Turkic world such as Azerbaijan, Kyrgyzstan, Turkmenistan and Bashkortostan in the Russian Federation - and several other periodicals.

In 1996 it established a bank, Asya Finans, operating on the basis of Islamic principles such as interest-free banking and initially tasked to raise investment funds for the newly-independent Turkic republics. Its activities are now extensive and global.

The network also spawned a Journalists and Writers Foundation, largely to facilitate dialogue activities, and a Teachers Foundation, each of which publishes journals and organizes symposiums and conferences - frequently abroad - and provides an umbrella for a host of dialogue groups and charitable organizations.

Cooperation between and overlapping membership of these various institutions is extensive and confusing - largely because Gulen-inspired institutions rarely own up to that fact. The websites of its schools, universities, media outlets, charities, and dialogue groups almost never directly refer to Gulen's inspiration.

Furthermore, the movement is loosely structured and decentralized, and each of its ventures are individually financed (and usually self-financing), and run on a voluntary basis by sympathizers with the network. The movement consists of numerous businessmen's associations, education trusts, and the like - each acting independently.

Nor does it have a membership as such, and Fethullahci are often loath to declare themselves openly as such. Indeed, the distinction between members, followers, sympathizers, and collaborators is blurred, and the movement is coy about revealing its scale - which it might not accurately know. As a consequence, estimates of the movement's "membership" vary considerably. One source suggested a figure anywhere between 200,000 and four million Turks.

More recently, "Prospect" magazine offered a figure of five million. This "structure," or lack of it, raises the question of whether so devolved, publicity-shy and voluntaristic a movement can exhibit the sense of purpose and discipline sometimes attributed to it, but it also adds to the suspicion with which it is regarded.

It is an internet-connected, informal and word-of-mouth set of overlapping networks that is more social movement than organization. It fuses faith with practical activity in a way that empirical and material analysis finds hard to grasp. It is undoubtedly well-resourced, interconnected, effective, and extensive, with tentacles throughout society and sympathizers within the political and bureaucratic elite. Indeed, Gulen sympathizers can increasingly be found in government service. A Turkish interior minister once suggested that as many as 70 percent of the nation's police force are Gulen sympathizers.

This is the kind of development that aggravates Turkey's secularists. After all, the judicial case against Gulen in the late 1990s was based on a tape in which he seemed to be urging his followers to take over the state by stealth. This chimes with the mission with which Gulen's "Golden Generation" is tasked--to re-Islamize society from below. Overall, the impression is of a parallel structure and society that sits uneasily alongside Turkey's officially secular state institutions and ruling elite, providing a silent, amorphous, and ungraspable challenge.

Educational activities

Overt religious teaching, and even explicit mention of Fethullah Gulen, is generally absent from Gulen educational establishments, both in Turkey and abroad. This is partly explained by the need to tread carefully in the presence of political authorities suspicious of religious (or on occasion for Gulen ventures abroad, foreign) activities.

It also reflects Gulen's educational philosophy, which stresses teaching "by example" and the cultivation of "good behavior" rather than religious devotion. In any case, matters of faith can be left to extra-curricula classes and the "mentoring" system, conducted by a teaching staff invariably made up of Gulen devotees. Gulen schools everywhere abide by local curricula, and both in Turkey and abroad they are immensely popular due to the strong reputation they have acquired for the quality of their technical and scientific teaching, for their English language instruction, and the high behavioral standards they set. This is true too of Gulen schools that serve the West's Turkish communities.

As a result, fees and entrance requirements are usually high, although schemes are sometimes in place for assisting able but poorer children. Around half of Gulen schools are located abroad, and of those the majority are found in Turkic Central Asia and Azerbaijan, where there are also half a dozen Gulen-sponsored universities and numerous other educational, welfare, and economic institutions and activities.

Indeed, the movement's focus is on Turkic communities, including those of the Russian Federation such as Dagestan, Karachay-Cherkessia, Tatarstan, and Bashkotorstan, and other former Soviet states containing Turkic or formerly Ottoman Muslim minorities such as Ukraine, Georgia, and Moldova, and in the Balkans. One can readily see why the movement targeted Turkic Central Asia and Azerbaijan for the main thrust of its activities. After all, many in Turkey's political class made a similar assessment of Turkish prospects in the region in the immediate aftermath of the Soviet collapse.

It shares a linguistic and ethnic root with Turkey, and a "folk Islam" that, as in Turkey, incorporates numerous Sufi sects and has absorbed pre-Islamic traditions, beliefs, and rituals. Furthermore, the Soviet era left behind a legacy of secular education and a commitment to science and modernity that broadly corresponds with the Gulen movement's aspirations.

The movement's activities in the wider Turkic world are additionally explained by its "commitment to Gulen's Turko-Islamic worldview." As one observer has expressed it, "...*the followers of the Gulen community aspire to reconnect Central Asians with their Turkic origins by spreading Turkish Muslim culture and morality to that region.*"

Even in Iraq, the Gulen schools' pupils are usually ethnic Turkmen, although Iraq's Turkmen are predominantly Shi'a rather than Sunni. Interestingly, Gulen has claimed that his movement was denied permission to open a school in an Azeri (Turkic) region of Iran due to Tehran's suspicion of its pan-Turkic aspirations.

Indeed, there may have been a greater receptivity to the "Turkism" of Gulen establishments located in Turkic regions rather than to their Islam. Turkish is used extensively, in addition to local languages where necessary. Furthermore, the overwhelming majority of the teachers and administrators in the movement's institutions abroad are Turks from Turkey rather than locals, although this could change as the movement spawns indigenous Gulen devotees.

As the movement has matured, so it appears to have shifted from its Turco-centrism to "*global educational activities that encourage the national identities of the countries in which it is operating.*" Today, Gulen schools and other educational establishments are globally far-flung, and can be found in locations as diverse as Russia, Armenia, the United States, Australia, China, Cambodia, sub-Saharan Africa, India, Pakistan, and in Western countries where Turkish minorities are located, notably Germany.

The intake of Gulen schools is mostly, though not exclusively, aimed at local Muslim populations. Interestingly though, even in decidedly non-Turkic countries such as India and in African states, portraits of Ataturk are on show, Turkish is taught, and the Turkish national anthem sung. Again, the Turkish-ness of Gulen schools seems more evident than their Islamism. This emphasis on Turkish language and culture has even won over some of the usually suspicious representatives of Turkey's secularist political class.

Some Gulen schools do not even have a majority Muslim intake, and might be located in zones of interreligious strife. Thus, in the

Philippines, in an area where the denominational split between Muslims and Christians is roughly half and half, a Gulen school employs many Filipino teachers (some of whom are Christian) and admits many Christian students.

Furthermore, and in keeping with the movement's commitment to interfaith dialogue, strong and healthy links are maintained with nearby Christian institutions. Even in Central Asia, non-Muslim students might be granted admission to Gulen establishments.

Interfaith Dialogue

Tracing the range of interfaith activities of the Gulen movement is difficult, given its devolved nature and its coy approach to self-publicity. The movement has sponsored or contributed to a confusing diversity of often overlapping interfaith organizations that operate both at the global or transnational and at the local intra societal level.

Unsurprisingly, the Gulen movement is seen by many non-Muslims as a particularly congenial Islamic dialogue partner. Amongst the numerous U.S.- based Gulen organizations are the Institute of Inter-Faith Dialog and the Inter-Faith Cultural Organization. The movement takes the credit for organizing the Inter-Civilization Dialogue Conference in 1997, and in 1998, it initiated the annual Eurasian Meetings, focusing on Central Asia and Russia.

It also claims to have provided the inspiration for the European Union Organization of Islamic Conference summit in Istanbul in 2002, in the wake of the September 11 attacks. In Turkey it has brought together leaders of the three Abrahamic religious communities, and initiated dialogues with Kurds and Alevis. Its activists and offices in Turkey have been subjected to threats and violent attacks in reaction to such endeavors.

Since its formation in 2007, the Intercultural Dialogue Center has functioned as a kind of clearing house for much of the movement's dialogue activity. It brings together a range of other dialogue platforms, such as the Abant Platform of the Journalists and Writers Foundations, the Intercultural Dialogue Platform, and the Dialogue Eurasia Platform.

In its various meetings, conferences, panels, publications, and other fora, these platforms seek to propagate Gulen's advocacy of tolerance and modernity, and bring together intellectuals, writers, activists, and others to discuss a wide range of current issues - some of them domestic. For example, early in 2007 Abant organized a panel in Turkey aimed at encouraging dialogue between the Sunni majority and the Alevi minority.

The Platform's first meeting was held in Abant in Turkey in 1998, but in 2004 it held its first annual meeting abroad, in Washington D.C., followed by Brussels and Paris. It was not until February 2007 that it held its first international meeting in the Islamic world, in Egypt.

Assessment

It is not possible to offer a definitive assessment of the Gulen movement's impact, either in Turkey or abroad. Its activities are too diverse both in their content and context, too devolved, and too disguised. Furthermore, the movement is a "work-in-progress," as it continues to evolve, expand, and influence. Much depends on the perspective one adopts.

Certainly in the Turkish context, the more one perceives the movement as a more-or-less hierarchical, disciplined, and "conspiratorial" organization that seeks to penetrate and undermine the Turkish state and society from within, the more one is inclined to adopt an essentially political interpretation of the movement's activities. This is precisely the model of the Gulen movement that many in Turkey's elite hold, and fear.

On the other hand, although the movement's lack of transparency and the weakness of its internal democracy and capacity for self-criticism are unsettling, this does not necessarily render it an extremist phenomenon. Neither Gulen nor the movement that takes his name is overtly politicized, and in the absence of hard evidence to the contrary, the movement will seem benign to many--unless of course one is ideologically opposed to challenges to Turkey's existing order, as many in Turkey are, or inherently uneasy about any faith-inspired movement.

A similar inconclusiveness emerges from an analysis of the movement's educational ventures. Although revenues raised by school fees are often used to enable access by less-privileged students, it remains an inescapable fact that the movement's educational model is elitist. In Turkey this is contributing to the creation of a parallel and Gulen-inspired elite.

In post-communist Central Asia, the main location of Gulen's overseas educational activities, successful applicants are usually the children either of the wealthy or of government officials. This has to be appreciated against the background of a collapsed educational, social, and economic infrastructure throughout much of the region. State spending on education has plummeted throughout the region, leading to school closures, a shortage of teachers, a degradation of the physical infrastructure, and widespread corruption surrounding school and college admissions and test results.

There is scope here for resentment of the "Turkish" schools. Although Gulen schools represent only around ten percent of Central Asia's education system, it could be that - in a tacit partnership with the Turkish state - the movement's activities will over the longer term intensify the emotive and material bonds between Turkic peoples - or their elites - and states.

The Gulen network's Central Asian elites could in time take on the forms of their Turkish counterparts, thereby encouraging the emergence of a pan-Turkic world linked by overlapping and fused identities. This could in turn ease the development of economic interactions, and even encourage closer state-to-state relationships.

Such an evolution would not quite accord with the kind of "Turkish model" that Ankara's secularists have sometimes hoped might be adopted in Central Asia, but it might dovetail with the pan-Turkic aspirations of nationalist elements in Turkey.

However, there are indications that a shared Turkic ethnic and linguistic root might not be sufficient to remove all barriers to a fuller interpenetration. The movement's educational establishments in the region are frequently referred to simply as "Turkish schools," and at least initially some local inhabitants seem to have resented the speed with which Turkish institutions replaced Soviet/Russian ones after 1991.

Furthermore, there have been indications of a distasteful Turkish chauvinism and "big brother" attitude toward the Turkic peoples of Central Asia. This sense of a "foreign" and intrusive penetration has occasionally combined with a dislike of the perceived missionary self-righteousness of the movement's teachers, whose piety and dedication can grate with more secular, non-believing and frequently dispossessed Central Asians.

In addition, the autocratic secularity of the region's political leaderships, and their post-Soviet sensitivity to anything they perceive as external meddling, puts the Gulen movement's reception in the Turkic world very much at the mercy of the region's governments. During the 1990s, Uzbek President Islam Karimov cracked down on the movement's activities in his country, including a ban on the distribution of Zaman.

The movement has minimal presence there today. It is unclear whether this was a reaction to the presence in his country of a religious group that he did not control, or whether it indicated retaliation against the Turkish state's harboring of Uzbek opposition leaders.

In 2005, Turkish teaching staff at the Islamic theology school at a university in Turkmenistan was sacked by the country's autocratic leader President Saparmurat Niazov. It seems that the Turkmen regime was becoming increasingly unhappy about both the pan-Turkic and Islamic ideology of the Gulen network in the country.

Beyond former Soviet Central Asia, the Taliban regime terminated the Gulen movement's activities in Afghanistan in the late 1990s owing to its disapproval both of its brand of Islam and of external interference in the country. Notwithstanding the movement's non-governmental status, incidents such as these can set back Ankara's relations with other states.

Assessments of the movement's educational activities in the non-Turkic world require a different approach. Although Gulen schools retain their elitism, receptivity to their "Turkish-ness" - the Turkish teachers, the Ataturk portraits, the learning of the Turkish language, and the singing of the Turkish anthem - will of course vary.

Perhaps the movement's activities in non-Turkic parts of the world might be likened to the work of the cultural agencies of the major globally - active Western powers such as the United States, the UK, and France. It is unlikely to do harm to Turkey's image and interests abroad, or to the more general cause of global understanding and tolerance.

On the other hand, the relative scale of the Gulen movement's presence is so small, and Turkey's broader military, political, technological and economic footprint in such regions so light, that it is hard to see what measurable good it might do either. Yet, again, it might be wise not to rush to judgment. After all, Turkey's global profile and "soft power" is expanding, and the existence of well-educated individuals with a knowledge of and sympathy with Turkish culture might further facilitate it. Perhaps too the movement has matured to the point that "activism through good deeds" is enough.

As Gulen schools host a primarily Muslim intake and its media outlets target primarily Muslim audiences, the movement's activities feed into its global contestation over what Islam is and what role it should play.

Gulen's teaching might increase Muslim receptivity to the idea of a Turkish-style fusion of modernity and Islam, and might generate local bulwarks against Islamist fundamentalism. Yet it is in precisely those regions most susceptible to fundamentalist Islamism that resistance to Gulen is at its strongest. In an apparent paradox, the Gulen movement's slightest presence is in the neighboring Arab and Iranian Muslim worlds.

This is explained by its occasionally dismissive attitude towards the practice of Islam in these countries, and by its pro-Turkic and somewhat anti-Arab attitude. General Arab mistrust of Turkey in particular, external interference in general, and suspicion of alternative forms of Islam, is in any case discouraging. Shi'i Iran's refusal to permit the establishment of (Sunni) Gulen schools in its (Turkic) areas has also ensured that barriers to the Gulen message remain in place.

Even so, overtures to the Arab and Iranian worlds occur, and may be intensifying. It appears that Gulen schools can now be found in Egypt, Jordan, Yemen, and Tunisia.

The relative absence of interaction with the Arab and Iranian worlds leads to an observation about the movement's global interfaith activities too. In the present atmosphere, the movement's championing of interfaith and inter-civilizational dialogue is surely welcome as an antidote to those who seem determined to prove Huntington right.

However, those engaged in interfaith dialogue are preaching largely to the converted--to each other. In a battle for hearts and minds, it is requisite to engage with precisely those variants of Islam that are disproportionately to be found in those areas of the world where the Gulen movement's footprint is at its lightest. Its venture into the Arab world, in the form of a Gulen-inspired Arabic magazine, Hira, first published in December 2005, and occasional meetings with like-minded Egyptian intellectuals, is unlikely to impress the region's radicals. On the other hand, this is a process - not an event - that produces winners and losers.

As such, it is not and may never be possible to assess definitively the impact of the Gulen movement's transnational interfaith engagement. Gulen schools in the West have served to reinforce or preserve Turkish and Muslim identities otherwise vulnerable to dilution as a result of interaction with host societies, although the simultaneous commitment to accommodation to and tolerance of host country customs is strong.

Whether such impulses are compatible is a moot point, of course. Overall though, the emphasis placed on integration in the Gulen's Turkish minority schools in the West, and the contribution to intercommunal relations where Gulen schools serve divided communities, perhaps permit a more positive assessment of the contribution the movement makes to more localized interfaith and intercommunal dialogue and tolerance.

Recep Tayip Erdogan

The scholar period

Erdoğan was born in Kasımpaşa, Istanbul. His family was descended from Georgian immigrants who settled from Batum to Rize. Erdoğan spent his early childhood in Rize before returning to Istanbul at the age of 13. He was educated at a religious Imam Hatip school and at Marmara University's Faculty of Economics and Administrative Sciences. Erdoğan played semi-professional football for 16 years.

The political carrier

In the 27 March 1994 local elections, Erdoğan was hand-picked by Erbakan for his oratory skills and was elected mayor with the party ticket. The Welfare Party became the largest party in Turkey for the first time, and Erdoğan became Mayor of Greater Istanbul as well as President of the Greater Istanbul Metropolitan Council.

As Mayor of Istanbul, he made a name for himself as a populist, effective administrator, building up Istanbul's infrastructure and transportation grid, while simultaneously beautifying the city, becoming one of Turkey's most popular politicians in the process. During this period Turkish Islamist politics entered a period of chaos.

Imprisonment

Erdoğan's pro-Islamist sympathies earned him a conviction in 1998. As the Istanbul Mayor, Erdogan was the most prominent mayor over 200 mayors and other officials in Turkey; because he was a national figure and hero to millions of Islamic-oriented voters, his case has focused attention.

In 1997, the Welfare Party was declared unconstitutional and was shut down on the grounds of threatening the secular nature of the state. In 1998, Erdoğan become a constant speaker at the meetings that was established by his friends from the banned Welfare Party.

There is no question that Erdogan is a pro-Islamist but the extent of his position regarding to basic characteristics of the state has been questioned on 12 December 1997 at a public meeting in Siirt in Eastern Anatolia. In his speech, Erdoğan identified the Turkish society as having "two fundamentally different camps" -- those who blindly follow the Atatürk's Reforms [seculars] and the Muslims who unite Islam with Sharia. He publicly read a well-known Islamic poem...

The AKP

The disbanded Welfare Party promptly reformed itself under a new name, the Virtue Party (Fazilet Partisi), which in turn was found unconstitutional on the same grounds in 1999.

Erdogan become the leader of a faction of moderate conservative members within the old Welfare Party, who formed the Justice and Development Party on August 14, 2001, in an attempt to ground moderate conservative politics in a secular democratic framework. Erdoğan, stated that "*AKP is not a political party with a religious axis.*" when the party was founded. On the other side, the traditionalists formed the Felicity Party (Saadet Partisi).

Privatization

Erdoğan's success story is keeping the economy on the track as designed by the Kemal Dervis. Erdoğan supported Ali Babacan, which Babacan continued to enforce the macro - economic policies of Kemal Dervis. Erdoğan did not cut the relations to international monitory control systems in favor of a national economy. The AK Party did quite well in almost all areas of the economy apart from the account deficit. Erdoğan said that during this premiership the economy's average growth rate was 7.3%, capita annual income had almost doubled, and all these were related to his economic reforms and the pursue of the membership of the European Union. However Erdogan's polices on unemployment figures were not effective.

Islamisation

Since Prime Minister Erdogan's AKP (Justice and Development Party) came to power in 2002, the rift between Turkey's secular circles and the government on many issues has deepened, often due to remarks by PM Erdogan himself.

Erdogan's statements on Turkish identity occupied the public agenda throughout December 2005. First, he defined Turkey's ethnic groups as its "sub-identities," with "citizenship in Turkey." His refusal to accept "Turkish" as the supra-identity of the people of Turkey, and his rejection of the concept of "the Turkish nation," sparked furious reactions from Turkey's secularist and nationalist circles.

Then, in response to a question about Turkey's Kurdish minority (during an official visit to New Zealand), Erdogan said that Turkey's dozens of ethnic groups were tied together by their shared religion - meaning Islam: "*Turkey is 99% Muslim, and above all, it is our religion that ties us all together.*" Upon his return to Turkey, he clarified his statements: "*I did not say that Islam is our supra-identity [as the media reported]. I said that Islam is the cement, and the most important factor, uniting our people.*"

While the Islamist media in Turkey hailed Erdogan's expression of these views, the secular media protested, stressing that the Turkish people's only higher identity was Turkish citizenship in the secular Turkish republic.

On December 10, Oktay Eksi wrote in Hurriyet: "*This is a friendly warning. [...] The ruling AKP government is following a very wrong and dangerous path. They [the AKP] are in an overall offensive against [our] secular Republic. They used to say, 'We respect the Law.' Then, when they were displeased with the law in Turkey, they carried it to the European Court of Human Rights [ECHR]. When they did not like the results of the Leyla Sahin case, they defied the ECHR and the law.*

"*They used to say that they respected science. Yet they launched an all-out war against the [Turkish] Higher Education Council and the universities. [...] In dealing with the European Union [membership] criteria, they kept saying 'one flag, one nation, one homeland' - but they changed, very quickly, 'one nation' into 'one ummet' [umma].*"

On the subject of Prime Minister Erdogan's definition of Islam as the "cement" of the people of Turkey, opposition CHP (Republican People's Party) member of parliament Ali Topuz was quoted in most of Turkey's mainstream newspapers: "[...] *If religion [Islam] is the cement of our people, what are we supposed to do about our non-Muslim minorities [and] the atheists? Are we going to exclude them from our nation? [...] The prime minister must remember that Ataturk brought us secularism, and absolute separation of state and religion is one of the most important principles of the Turkish revolution. [...] I call on the prime minister to demonstrate political maturity.*"

On December 18, 2005 Hayrettin Karaman wrote in the Islamic daily Yeni Safak: "[...] *Being a Muslim demands the subordination of tribalism (which corresponds to nationalism in today's language) to the unity of Islamic brotherhood. Islam comes above all other ties. [...] When the Islamic nation (umma) is united, no Muslim individual or group will be left out; they will be part of it. [...] According to the Lausanne treaty, only the non-Muslims are recognized as minorities in Turkey.*"

On December 11, Murat Bardakci wrote in the secular mass-circulation daily Hurriyet: "[...] *If what the prime minister said were true, and that religion was such an important uniting factor, how come we [Turks], during the collapse of the Ottoman Empire, were bitterly betrayed by Muslims [...] and why was it that the [bloody] uprisings during the initial years of our republic were by the [rebelling] religious [Muslims]? [...]*

In 1914, at the outset of the [First] World War, wasn't it Hussein, the sharif of Mecca, who issued the fatwas against the Ottoman Sultan-Caliph Reshad inciting all Arabs to a rebellion that painted the Muslim lands with the blood of tens of thousands of [our] sons? [...] In 1925, Sheikh Said issued calls from southeast Anatolia to arm and attack the Turks: [...] '...Capture their soldiers, [...] the infidel Turks' cannons, the Turks' guns [...]. Your guide is Mohammed, your helper is Allah. You are many times stronger than their government [in Ankara] [...] Save and protect the sanctity of Islam [...]'"

Prior to the 2002 election, the AKP promised its Islamic electorate that it would end the ban on Islamic headscarves in the universities, and that the graduates of Turkey's Imam Hatip religious schools would be accepted into the universities.

However, once in office, the ruling AKP could not deliver on these promises to its religious base, mainly because of the strong opposition on the part of Turkey's strictly secular Higher Education Council that governs the policies of Turkey's state universities. The conflict deepened with the recent arrest and incarceration of the president of Yuzuncu Yil University (YYU) in Van, Professor Yucel Askin, for alleged procedural misconduct.

The Turkish media is suggesting that Prof. Askin's incarceration was an attempt by the Islamic government to remove a secular republican president from a university that was known, until he took office in 1999, as a hotbed for Islamists. During his tenure, Prof. Askin put an end to the activities of various Islamic extremists at the university.

All Turkey's university presidents, as well as the Higher Education Council and members of the Turkish Bar Associations, strongly protested Prof. Askin's arrest, and claimed that Turkey's judiciary system was being manipulated by the government. On October 22, 2005, 74 presidents and vice-presidents of Turkish universities flew to Van to visit Prof. Askin in prison, in a show of solidarity, and held a meeting at YYU. A declaration by the Board of Presidents of YOK read: "Defending President Askin means defending our Republic." Higher Education Council head Professor E. Tezic and the 74 presidents were met by a number of protesters in Van, who shouted "Allahu Akbar."

Soon after their visit to Van, President of the Turkish Republic Ahmet N. Sezer invited all the university presidents to his October 29 Republic Day Reception, further angering Prime Minister Erdogan, who earlier had said about the solidarity visit, "Those who go to Van [i.e. the university presidents] should mind their own businesses and not interfere with legal matters."

Erdogan on Secularism:

"If the people want it, of course secularism will go away. You cannot rule this people by force; you don't have the power to do that. This [i.e. secularism] cannot work in spite of the people. And anyway, for the love of Allah, what is this secularism? You ask them to define it. They can't. They say that it varies from place to place. So what sort of a strange thing is this [secularism]? Today, for every concept there is a definition in the dictionary. Every concept must have a definition [...]

The interior minister comes and says that the state can interfere with religion. What about the rest? Why don't you say the rest? No! He does not say that the religion can interfere with the state. Yesterday I was at the Bosphorus University; and some of the - probably impressionable - young people there asked me, 'Mr. Mayor, what do you think about secularism? There are concerns that secularism is disappearing. What will happen?' This is what I said to those young friends:

'In the West they say, Render unto Caesar the things which are Caesar's, and unto God the things that are God's. But this country's interior minister says that Caesar has rights but God does not!' But the fact is that 99% of the people of this country are Muslims. You cannot be both secular and a Muslim! You will either be a Muslim, or secular! When both are together, they create reverse magnetism [i.e. they repel one another]. For them to exist together is not a possibility! Therefore, it is not possible for a person who says 'I am a Muslim' to go on and say 'I am secular too.' And why is that? Because Allah, the creator of the Muslim, has absolute power and rule!"

Erdogan on Turkish Constitution:

"As for [the motto of Turkish democracy] 'Sovereignty belongs unconditionally to the people.' Now, look here. This is a lie! And it's a huge lie! We [former PM Erbakan's Islamist RP (Welfare) Party] suggested this to them for their constitution: We said 'Let's put brackets next to 'sovereignty belongs unconditionally to the people' and write within the brackets, 'once every five years.'

They began to laugh. I asked them why they were laughing. Do the people have such a privilege, other than once every five years? Then what's-his-name says - and where does he say this? - it is in 1985 and we are having a discussion on the constitution in a meeting in the Marmara Hotel. He gets up and says 'No, this is not right.'

At that moment, the former finance minister, who was completely drunk, also joins in to give advice. I told them that they must have prepared this constitution at the same table [at which they together *consume alcohol]. Why? Because they do not prepare these constitutions with sober heads, but with drunken heads! That is why their constitutions last no more than two years.*

Now, this constitution is full of gaps and holes. Like a rag with patches. The other day journalists asked me what I think about this [constitution]. I said, Look, what do they say? That sovereignty belongs unconditionally to the people. You must think well. When [does the sovereignty belong to the people]? It is only when they go to the polls [every five years] that sovereignty belongs to the people. But both materially, and in essence, sovereignty unconditionally and always belongs to Allah!"

Erdogan and the women

Speaking at a conference in Istanbul entitled "Woman and Politics," Emine Erdogan, the wife of Prime Minister Recep Tayyip Erdogan, said that women are inevitable participants in politics as in life. *"Our women have to undertake responsibilities in politics just as they have at home,"* said Erdogan. Commenting on the number of candidates fielded by her husband's ruling Justice and Development Party (AKP) for upcoming local elections, Erdogan called the number regrettably inadequate, adding that the prime minister felt the same way.

War is declared

The first breaking point was the so-called "MIT (Turkish National Intelligence Organization) crisis." In February 2012, MIT head Hakan Fidan, a confidant of Erdogan, was called by an Istanbul prosecutor to testify as part of an investigation into the Kurdistan Workers Party (PKK).

This was, as The New York Times then reported, *"the latest round in a power struggle between the country's security forces and its intelligence agency."* It was also widely interpreted as a power struggle between pro-Gulen police/judiciary and the AKP. Since then, Erdogan's supporters complain of a "parallel state" within the state, which allegedly acts according its own internal hierarchy and uses state power for its own purposes.

Since the "MIT crisis" of February 2012, the AKP-Gulen movement relations have been silently sour. But in mid-November 2013, all hell broke lose when Erdogan planned to close down "prep schools," or weekend courses that prepare high school students for university exams. Since about a quarter of these schools are operated by the Gulen movement, and are a source of both finance and recruitment, the movement perceived this move as an attack. The pro-Gulen media opposed the government's "attack on private enterprise." The government responded with harsh statements, and the war of words was soon declared an "open war."

The prep schools

The spark that fueled the war was a scoop that the Zaman daily, the flagship of the Gulenist media, published coverage on Nov. 13 about a draft law indicating that the AKP is readying to close down the prep schools in the 2013-14 school year.

University and secondary school admissions in Turkey are determined through nationwide centralized exams, since the total number of students hugely outnumbers school capacity. The fierce competition has been coupled with a chronic quality deficit at public schools. Thus, the establishment and growth of private schools preparing students for the exams has become inevitable.

The Hizmet (Service) movement — or the Gulen community, as it is widely known in Turkey — owes its domestic clout mainly to the thousands of prep and regular schools it began to open in the 1980s. Since then, it has grown into a global sociopolitical Islamic movement thanks significantly to the schools it also opened around the world. Closing the prep schools by law would no doubt deal a major blow to the community. There is also a social aspect to the issue, given that the prep schools employ about 100,000 people.

According to Zaman, the prep schools will have to be converted to regular high schools or face closure, if the draft law is passed in its current form. The daily says only 263 of the existing 3,100 prep schools could transform themselves to high schools, which means that the overwhelming majority would have to close. Those which do not comply with the law would face heavy fines of at least 500,000 Turkish lira ($250,000).

The Sabah daily, known to be close to the AKP, responded to Zaman on Nov. 15 with a front-page story, titled "Black propaganda about prep schools." The education minister branded the Zaman report "a campaign of obvious lies and provocation."

The same day, Zaman appeared with a front-page headline that declared the law to be "unprecedented even in military coup eras." Later in the day, an audio recording of the community's spiritual leader, Fethullah Gulen, was released on the hergul.org web site, which routinely carries his talks. Gulen, too, likened the closure plan to the oppression of military coup eras. *"We've been through that since the 1960 coup; we've been slapped in the face. We've been through the 1970 coup and got kicked. We've been through the 1980 coup and got kicked again. But the scores are now being settled with those who slapped and kicked us,"* he said.

Gulen was widely thought to be likening the government to a "pharaoh" in his ensuing remarks. *"If people concerned with mundane interests in every realm are against you, if the Pharaoh is against you, if Croesus is against you, then you are walking on the right path. … It's very important to clench your teeth when calamities are coming down on you like a sledgehammer,"* he said. The community, meanwhile, is waging an extensive social media campaign against the closing of the prep schools.

It should be noted that the prep schools were not a matter of public debate in Turkey. The people had no negative perception of or complaints against those institutions. Thus, it was not possible to argue that the government's plan to shut the schools was a move to meet a popular demand. So, the only other argument was that the government's motivation was to punish the Gulen community.

Government ministers have so far reacted in a low-key manner to the community's indignation. In a TV interview on Nov. 14, Education Minister Nabi Avci denied they were working on a draft law like the one reported by Zaman, saying that the objective was to gradually transform the prep schools into high schools. Deputy Prime Minister Bekir Bozdag, for his part, said the issue was not a hastily decided step but has been on the government's agenda for three years.

The Corruption probe

The investigations made public on Dec. 17, 2013 revealed the biggest corruption and bribery scandal in the history of the republic, in which some members of the Justice and Development Party (AK Party) government as well as family members of President Recep Tayyip Erdoğan were allegedly implicated.

The investigations were, however, stalled by the president and prominent figures in the government. Since the investigations were made public in December 2013, Erdoğan has sought to discredit the prosecutors and policemen behind the investigations by accusing them of working to oust the AK Party from power. The prosecutors and policemen -- along with tens of thousands of others -- have already been displaced.

The investigations are known as efforts by the judiciary and the police force to fight a corruption ring made up of ministers, bureaucrats and businessmen. The amounts of money involved in the alleged activities of the corruption ring register in the ballpark of billions of dollars. The investigations into corruption, tender-rigging, unlawful gains and bribery allegations began in March 2012. They were led by prosecutors Celal Kara and Muammar Akkaş. Both were eventually removed from the cases.

The alleged crimes -- as mentioned by the prosecutors -- include: *"The transfer of lands with a value of billions of dollars at very low prices, seizure of mines from businessmen by force, tender-rigging, illegally giving state tenders worth billions of dollars to businessmen, changing the status of protected areas through bribery, opening these up to construction and making giant profits off of them."*

It all started on Dec. 17, 2013. Turkey was shaken by early morning police raids that resulted in the detention of the sons of three now-former ministers, a state bank manager, a mayor and high-profile businessmen with close ties to the government. Among the businessmen was Reza Zarrab, an Iranian living in Turkey. Some of the suspects were arrested -- albeit briefly -- after the operation.

Zarrab was accused of managing a network used to launder at least 87 billion euros to circumvent international sanctions against Iran. In addition, he allegedly bribed ministers, their sons and public officials to keep his network working.

According to prosecutors' findings, Zarrab distributed TL 139 million in bribes. Around TL 11 million of this sum allegedly went to former Economy Minister Zafer Çağlayan's son, Salih Kaan Çağlayan. The investigation details also revealed that former Interior Minister Muammer Güler received a $5 million bribe from Zarrab in exchange for granting Turkish citizenship to the Iranian businessman on exceptional grounds. Furthermore, Minister Çağlayan was accused of accepting a valuable watch worth 300,000 Swiss francs (TL 700,000) as a bribe from Zarrab.

In addition, police found $4.5 million in cash stuffed into shoeboxes and about TL 10 million also in cash in a bookshelf in now-former Halkbank General Manager Süleyman Arslan's house. Zarrab allegedly sent 500,000 euros in bribes to former EU Affairs Minister Egemen Bağış. In addition, former Environment and Urban Planning Minister Erdoğan Bayraktar was accused of paving the way for building contractors to obtain illegal profits.

On Dec. 25, three ministers resigned from their posts while one other was removed from the Cabinet. Bayraktar publicly said that Erdoğan, who was prime minister at the time, should also quit, as most of the amendments to construction plans in environmentally protected zones mentioned in the corruption investigation were made on Erdoğan's orders.

Also on Dec. 25, 2013 the İstanbul Chief Public Prosecutor's Office ordered the detention of 30 suspects. Around $100 billion in bribes were said to be involved in the case. Among the main suspects of the investigation was Erdoğan's son, Bilal, businessmen Mehmet Cengiz and Latif Topbaş and Yasin al-Qadi, a Saudi Arabian businessman who is on the US Treasury Department's "Specially Designated Global Terrorist" list.

The İstanbul Police Department, which saw an extensive purge of its top officers following the Dec. 17 corruption operation, did not comply with the order, however. Shortly after the order, prosecutors involved in the Dec. 25 investigation were removed from office on the grounds that they had abused their authority. The government assigned new prosecutors to the investigation in an apparent move to drop charges against corruption suspects.

Bilal Erdoğan was accused of receiving unlawful donations at the Foundation of Youth and Education in Turkey (TÜRGEV), on whose executive board he sits. TÜRGEV is at the center of the corruption investigation, which includes serious allegations of bribery and irregularities within the foundation. Prosecutors involved in the probe claimed that Bilal Erdoğan abused his father's influence to help TÜRGEV purchase valuable land in several provinces at prices far below market value. Various news reports have emerged over the past few months detailing the how certain plots of land and recreational facilities have been donated to TÜRGEV by certain municipalities.

Since Dec. 17,2013 Erdoğan has claimed the corruption investigations were a coup attempt by influential international groups and their proxies in Turkey to topple the AK Party government. He praised Zarrab for his contribution to the country's economy and charity events.

In addition, he targeted the "parallel structure," a clear reference to sympathizers of the faith-based Hizmet movement inspired by Turkish Islamic scholar Fethullah Gülen. He said the corruption probes were orchestrated by the movement to oust the government.

He declared a "war" against Hizmet and ordered the arbitrary reassignment of bureaucrats, members of the judiciary and the police force, who he believes are followers of the Hizmet movement. The number of reassigned officials now exceeds 40,000. The fact that no internal investigation had been launched before those officials were reassigned and that most of them were not given any explanation for their reassignment has led to comments that the government -- per Erdoğan's orders -- is carrying out a witch hunt against its critics.

Erdoğan virtually confessed to carrying out a witch hunt in a public address in May. When commenting on the reassignments, he -- without providing any evidence whatsoever -- accused the reassigned officers of "betraying Turkey" for their suspected links to the faith-based Hizmet movement, which he currently views as "enemy number one."

"If reassigning individuals who betray this country is called a witch hunt, then, yes, we will carry out a witch hunt," Erdoğan said. However, he has yet to give a satisfactory explanation about a number of leaked documents and voice recordings that suggest he, his family members and some government officials have engaged in unlawful activities.

In one of the recordings, Erdoğan and his son Bilal are allegedly heard talking about a plan how to get rid of huge sums of money stashed at several houses during the Dec. 17 corruption operation. Erdoğan, at the beginning of the recorded conversations, briefs Bilal about the operation and asks him to "zero" the money by distributing it among several businessmen. Towards the end of the conversations, Bilal tells his father that he and others have *"finished the tasks you gave us,"* implying that the whole sum was "zeroed."

Erdoğan dismissed the authenticity of the recordings, saying they were doctored. However, official documents by the National Police Department suggest that the recordings are authentic. In another recorded conversation, Erdoğan was allegedly heard accepting two villas from businessman Mustafa Latif Topbaş in return for easing zoning restrictions in İzmir's Urla district.

Last but not least, Erdoğan is accused of helping Yasin al-Qadi, a Saudi businessman listed as a terror financier by international organizations, enter Turkey several times even though al-Qadi had been banned by the Cabinet from entering the country.

Former İstanbul Police Department financial crimes unit head Yakup Saygılı, who was placed under arrest on Thursday after being detained for carrying out the Dec. 17 and 25 operations, said during his testimony to the police that al-Qadi entered Turkey several times thanks to Erdoğan's security guards when Erdoğan was prime minister. According to Saygılı, al-Qadi could not have entered Turkey without the help and influence of Erdoğan. In addition, Saygılı said, al-Qadi was provided with a false passport to enter Turkey and a villa to use during his stay in the country.

The Coup

A major difficulty in understanding the Gülenists' endgame and their involvement in the coup d'etat derives from the group's ontology. Outsiders are confused about their organization and methods of operation due to their secretive nature, cult-like operation, cell-based structure, strict hierarchy, and extensive use of dissimulation.

However, for those whose life ever crossed paths with that of the group (regardless of the extent of this conjunction), the Gülenist methodology of recruitment and infiltration is common knowledge. It is for certain that they have been laying the groundwork for a complete takeover of the state for decades. Considering the ranks of the captured military officers including the generals, one could argue that the terror organization has been operating within the Turkish army with varying capacity at least since the mid-1980s. They have been following three main strategies to expand their influence and operational capabilities in the army: infiltration, conversion, and the formation of alliances.

Although for many it was common knowledge, the July 15 coup attempt proved beyond all doubt that the Gülenists had not only infiltrated the army. It became clear that they considered the civil bureaucracy, the judiciary, and NGOs as means to expand their influence over the state and Turkish society. Yet, the military occupied a special spot in the group's list of priorities.

This is primarily because Fetullah Gülen has an interesting affinity with the coups and junta regimes which he believes have the ultimate say in Turkish politics despite years of democratization especially during the AK Party era. For example, after a literary overture to the 1980 Coup, Gülen described it as a resurrection and the last outpost of the nation's expectations and saluted the army with high praises.

He praised one of the chief architects of the February 28 "post-modern" coup d'etat, Çevik Bir, in a letter he penned in late 1997. Despite the rising power of civilian politics under the AK Party rule, the Gülenists came to believe that the armed forces are still at the center of gravity and if other attempts fail, a takeover via the armed forces could be a last resort.

One of the centerpieces of the Gülenist strategy of expansion and control has been training students from secondary school onwards for the military high school exams. Sharp students often from economically disadvantaged backgrounds are selected by the group, and the group elders initially socialize, indoctrinate and train them in apartments reserved only for the military high school candidates. In the earlier years, it is probable that there was a greater emphasis on the students' mental and physical qualities. However, as the group expanded their influence within the armed forces and started to occupy key positions, such as the offices related to military recruitment, they became less selective given that they had already gained more influence over the recruitment process in the armed forces.

The students who succeed in entering the armed forces are already indoctrinated by their contact person who uses their code names rather than their real ones. The aide-de-camp of the Chief of General Staff Levent Turkkan explains this process clearly in his confessions. He explained that he comes from a poor farmer's family, and the Gülenists first contacted him when he was a secondary school student.

He also confessed that he was given the exam questions the night before the exam at a house owned by Gülenists, and after his admission to the Işıklı Military High School, he continued his covert ties with the group and followed orders coming from the group, including wiretapping the then Chief of General Staff Necdet Özel.

The Gülenists also shape the students' personal lives in an effort to preserve their ties to the group. In this sense, the students pray secretly and limit their ties with their families; the Gülenists even have a say regarding the women they should marry. These actions remove any morsel of doubt regarding the involvement of Gülenists with these students. Once they are in the armed forces, they follow orders from the group and at the same time try carefully to convert un-affiliated students in to Gülenist militants.

The Gülenists try to convert military school students as well as army officers. The students already indoctrinated by the Gülenists, as is the case in civilian life, socialize with potential recruits at school and outside. When a student is deemed ready for the next step, he is introduced to an elder contact person outside the school and invited to a house used by the Gülenists as a cell. He is then gradually indoctrinated using similar methods to those used in the secondary school years. These efforts of conversion are sometimes exerted in periods beyond school years as well; apparently there were group militants who were converted in later periods of their lives through friendships and marriages.

The Gülenists are also known for forging alliances with individuals who are pragmatists and have personal agendas that can be furthered by an alliance with the group. For many officers in the armed forces, the Gülenists are known as a strong clique that is influential in key decisions within the armed forces regarding issues such as promotions. Thus, an alliance with or submission to the Gülenist clique within the army had direct implications for their carrier…

Although the Gülenists have been in the headlines due to the coup attempt of July 15, it should be noted that this was not their first attempt at total or partial takeover - obviously, however, it was the first one mobilizing their militant followers in the armed forces and using them to take full control of the state.

In expectation of the High Military Council's meeting where a great purge of Gülenist officers was expected, the Gülenists rushed to execute a preemptive strike against the government. The attempt failed yet again and has already prompted an even more extensive purge of the Gülenists from the armed forces as well as from other government sectors.

Back then

Turkey's political history has undergone many interruptions due to myriad coups. In 1960, 1971, 1980, 1997 and 2007, we were subjected to military interventions; we have been told for years that "Turkey's political history is the history of coups." Tanks would head to the streets, they would seize public buildings, the state radio and television would broadcast a "coup announcement," and finally, state and government officials would be arrested and a new era would begin.

Exceptionally, it was in 2007 that Turkey saw for the first time that civilian politicians could frustrate a military intervention and repel the army. In 2007, a controversial statement was released on the website of the Turkish Armed Forces. It came to be known as the 'e-memorandum,' and aimed at intervening in the Turkish presidential elections. Then, the government authorities took the necessary steps, made counter-statements, reminded the true place of the army in a democratic country and thus obstructed a military intervention in Turkish politics.

What happened

On July 15 at 9:48 p.m., a news portal sent a 'breaking news' message from its social media account: *"Troops in front of Beylerbeyi Palace: Martial law declared. Everybody, go home!"* The message was familiar for someone who knows the history of military coups in Turkey. Interestingly, the sender of the message was familiar too. The message was posted on a website called Haberdar, one of the Gülen Organization's media bases. After the announcement, the website started to post articles trying to prove that the military had carried out *"a successful coup in the chain of command."*

Precisely 12 minutes after the news outlet shared the "successful coup" message, it was heard that tanks were positioned to cut off traffic on the Boğazici and Fatih Sultan Mehmet bridges in İstanbul, and in a few minutes people began to share the information that warplanes were flying low over Ankara. Soon it was heard that helicopters were opening fire on the headquarters of the Turkish Armed Forces and the National Intelligence Organization (MIT), both in Ankara. Police and troops began to clash around public buildings in different parts of the country. Less than 30 minutes after the coup announcement, claims that the Ataturk Airport in İstanbul was besieged by tanks and that the control tower had been seized by the pro-coup soldiers began to circulate.

From the very moment that rumors of "soldiers attempting a coup" began spreading on social media and photos of the tanks placed at the entrance of the two bridges in İstanbul were shared, clear messages were broadcasted by the Turkish authorities. Before the coup plotters got a chance to force TRT (Turkish Radio and Television) to read the coup announcement, Prime Minister Binali Yıldırım went live on A Haber at 11:05 p.m. and said that a group of soldiers within the Turkish Armed Forces had undertaken an unlawful attempt to seize control, but that the government was on duty and the citizens must protect democracy. He tenaciously highlighted that the coup attempt was being executed outside the chain of command. TV channels started announcing that a junta led by the Gülen Organization was behind the coup attempt.

By the time the pro-coup terrorists seized the TRT building and forced the anchorwoman to read the coup announcement at gunpoint, the atmosphere that they had planned to create could no longer exist. People already knew that *"they were faced by a terrorist organization nested in the Turkish Armed Forces."* Thus, the coup plotters were firstly defeated in the media war.

But the essential move that thwarted the coup attempt came from President Recep Tayyip Erdoğan, who joined a live broadcast on CNN Türk via videophone and called on the Turkish public to stand up against the coup plotters, to defend democracy and foil the coup.

Erdoğan implicated the Gülenist factions within the army in initiating the attempt and clearly underlined that the government was in charge. This call was enough to make people take to the streets. Thousands of civilians all around Turkey showed great courage by crowding the streets, filling up public squares, walking on tanks, and taking the guns of the pro-coup soldiers from their hands. Civilians not only crowded the streets, but also provided moral support to the government's legitimate security forces. The people's determination encouraged the security forces to fight more decisively against the pro-coup terrorists wearing soldier uniforms.

That night, Turkey experienced one of the biggest crises in the history of its democracy. Even though Turkey has experienced military coups and barbarous attacks by terrorist organizations before, this was the first time that the country faced an attempt by a terrorist organization that had infiltrated the state. This attempt was managed by a "cleric" residing in the American state of Pennsylvania, whose followers see him not as an ordinary person but as a messianic figure. Following his lead, the Gülen Organization (FETÖ) mobilized its cells in the Turkish Armed Forces (TAF) and attempted to plunge a dagger into the heart of Turkey's democracy.

Modus Operandi

Considering the military units that took part in the action on the night of July 15, the junta planned to mobilize a large number of military troops. A big part of the commando and combatant brigades, almost all of the airbases and the whole of the naval forces except the submarine flotilla, were planned to be set in motion.

The Gülenist members, a small but influential faction within the Turkish Armed Forces, resorted to brutal force and used violent means to crack the people's resistance. Coup plotters ran over people with tanks; deliberately opened fire on selected civilians; closed down the Bosporus and Fatih Sultan Mehmet bridges in İstanbul; captured the Ataturk Airport and canceled the flights; they raided the official state television TRT, and forced a "coup memorandum" that was clearly a reminiscent of the Sept. 12, 1980 coup to be read on live TV.

They attempted to seize the Justice and Development Party's (AK Party) provincial centers. Moreover, they tried to assassinate the president and the prime minister; bombed the Turkish Grand National Assembly; attacked the Turkish General Staff of Military, the National Intelligence Organization (MIT), the Police Special Operations Center, and the Police Academy in Ankara with the state's guns and bombs in an attempt to topple the democratically-elected, legitimate government.

The most striking difference being that, the plotters used terrorizing means such as opening fire against the people in the streets from tanks and helicopters. Unfortunately, more than two hundred civilians and security personnel lost their lives resisting the coup, and more than two thousand were injured.

Following the reactions from different ranks and branches of the army, it was understood that the plotters violated the chain of command and the commanders-in-chief of the armed forces and the rest of the army did not take part in the coup attempt. Therefore it appeared to be an attempt by a small faction from the very early hours and President Erdoğan stated that the coup attempt was controlled by Gulen Organization.

Relying on the information revealed on July 16, the aides of the President, Chief of Staff, and of the Commanders of the armed forces all took part in the junta together with the soldiers on active duty who hold critical positions such as intelligence and information services units. A crucial point here is that the junta met with resistance in almost all of these units.

Three-stage plan

Later on it was revealed that even the most minimal amount of resistance had a significant negative impact on the conduct of the coup attempt. In operational terms, the junta operated within the frame of a three-stage plan. The first stage was to take control of the headquarters of army general staff. The second stage was designed to obtain the control in the whole country. The third one was to declare martial law and to establish the political and social order anew. When each stage is looked at individually, it is possible to find clues on how the coup process would proceed and on why it would eventually fail.

In the first stage, the target was to gain the control of the headquarters of army general staff. To this end, the Chief-of-Staff and the Commanders of the Armed Forces were taken hostage. The main purpose here was to stage the coup, first of all, in the chain of command. This was the reason why forcible attempts were made to make the Chief of Staff and the Commanders sign the declaration prepared by the usurpers.

However the resistance they faced made it impossible. Despite that, the junta did not renounce their attempt, retained the top rank of the army, and tried to take control of the military headquarters. The counteraction of the First Army against the junta on the ground was the most visible sign of this non-compliance. In addition many high ranking commanders went live on TV declaring that they are against any coup attempt. That hindered the full control of the junta on the general staff HQ.

The second stage was designed to gain the control on the ground in the whole country. To this end the junta deployed tanks to strategic locations such as the Bosphorus Bridge, Atatürk Airport, and İstanbul Metropolitan Municipality. Simultaneously the troops listed above took action. Taking the control of the strategic points and institutions in Ankara and İstanbul was very significant. That's why they intervened at the National Intelligence Organization and the units of Security General Directorate with artillery.

The special operation command in Gölbaşı and security general directorates in Ankara and İstanbul were the first targets. An attempt to take over the Special Forces Command of the Army was also made. However in all of these points, there was a strong resistance against the rebel groups. Therefore from the very first moment, the junta faced a swift resistance in all of the points it tried to take control of, particularly in the Headquarters of the General Command.

At the same time, the junta made a move to neutralize President Recep Tayyip Erdoğan. In a program at CNN International, Erdoğan said that "it was an attempt of assassination or detainment; I escaped in the last instance" adding that two of his guards were martyred. The junta's inability to detain and neutralize Erdoğan, who is both President and the Chief Commander, became a turning point for the failure of the coup attempt.

Another attempt of the junta was directed at media channels; in order to make the declaration of a coup and psychologically have the upper hand, media control is essential. In this regard, the control of the national channel TRT and the reading of the coup declaration from there were important to the junta and they succeeded in doing that. Contrary to the expected practice of reading of the coup declaration by junta members, they forced a speaker to read it.

However as it was featured only in one TRT channel, it did not have a significant psychological impact. The appearance of the President, the Prime Minister, Ministers, Top Commanders, and several high rank officials on other TV channels ensured that the junta failed to take control over the public through the media.

Failure of the coup

The failure of the coup attempt can be evaluated through four factors. First is the popular resistance against the coup, second is the powerful political leadership and the third one is the operational activity. While these three factors formed the resistance bloc, the media is the fourth factor which broadcasted in compliance with the three resisting actors.

The very first sign of the coup was the closing of the two bridges in İstanbul by tanks. People, who suspected a coup as a result of the closing, began to gather in the critical points occupied by the junta forces and intervened in the situation. The popular resistance in the critical locations such as airports, bridges, security headquarters and the Presidential Campus precluded the juntai activity from succeeding. Furthermore, the resistance of the people that never ceased, even under the heavy gunfire of the junta forces, contributed to the gaining of the upper hand by the security forces.

The active popular resistance also helped in the gaining of the psychological edge. The stance of the people despite the reading of the coup declaration on TRT and taking back control of TRT from the junta forces provided one of the most critical victories to the civilian resistance. In brief, the people used all the opportunities available to thwart the coup attempt without resorting to arms and without harming public or private properties, displaying an effective performance of civilian resistance.

The second factor has been Erdoğan's appearance on TV at the most critical moments of the coup attempt stating that he stands against the coup by any means and calling people out onto the streets to protect the Turkish democracy was significant from two aspects. Firstly that provided a strong motivation to the people resisting the coup. His appearance fused the different anti-coup groups together for the sole purpose: to bring about the failure of the coup attempt.

The second factor that reversed the crisis in the early hours was Erdoğan's taking the risk of flying to İstanbul while the junta F16 war planes were in-flight. With his coming to İstanbul, the civilian initiative and the operational units on the ground united with the political leadership. In addition to that the integrated actions of the cabinet members and the President, was important for managing the process efficiently.

Prime Minister Binali Yıldırım, as well as other ministers, went live on the TV and openly declared that they will stand against the coup resulting in the mobilization of the public. The support from the leader of the Nationalist Movement Party, Devlet Bahçeli also had a significant contribution to the popular resistance in the streets.

The third factor that hindered the coup attempt was the mobilization of security units. Together with the Special Operations Unit, mobilization of all the facilities of internal security organizations provided a capacity to counter the junta forces. The resistance of most of the units in the Turkish Army, primarily that of the Special Forces Unit, and the public statements of the army high-ranks against the coup attempt, helped people to realize the exaggerated capacity of the junta and contributed to the decisiveness of the resisting groups. The rescue of the Turkish Chief of Staff and the Commanders-in-Chief of the armed forces by the Special Forces Unit were significant for regaining the ground control.

The coming together of these three factors into one bloc drew the media over to that side. The broadcast of the popular resistance and not supporting the coup attempt in Ankara and İstanbul from the very initial moments had a high motivational impact over the people. The negation of the enforcedly read coup declaration at TRT, or partial coverage of it in other channels exposed an important deficit of the junta: They could control neither the ground nor the media. Withdrawal from the raided buildings of TRT and Doğan Media Group showed that the anti-coup bloc had the upper hand.

The dissent toward Erdoğan, which has been consumed by opposition groups for a while, was the main factor that misled the coup attempters. The coup plotters exaggerated the effect of this factor and were caught by its illusion. They assumed that the Justice and Development Party (AK Party) dissidents would unite for the coup. They hoped they would meet overt or covert support of various societal segments if they could form a dissident alliance with the army. They thought secular, leftist, nationalist or Alevi citizens would take to the streets to support the coup.

After the failure of the attempted coup, we started to learn about the number of generals and commanders who participated, which further shocked Turkish public opinion. Although many thought that military personnel served to protect the homeland, some of them were actually planning to overthrow the democratically-elected government and were prepared to do whatever was necessary to achieve this goal, even if that meant killing civilians.

After these arrests, there are many questions regarding the actions of these coup actors. The extent of the investigation is not clear, but considering that some of the commanders who supported the coup were stationed and commanded in critical regions and were responsible for sensitive matters, it is important to review whether they tried to do something earlier to sabotage the government or neglected their duties, before their support for military interventions.

Gulen and CIA

Central Asia, with its vast energy wealth, is of major interest to US oil and gas companies. The region is also of key strategic interest in the 'Great Game' as Russia, China and the US compete for dwindling energy supplies. The US government has been using Turkey as a proxy to gain control over Central Asia via Pan-Turkic nationalism and religion.

Green Card

In a recent immigration court case involving Turkish Islamic Leader, Fethullah Gulen, US prosecutors exposed an illegal, covert, CIA operation involving the intentional Islamization of Central Asia. This operation has been ongoing since the fall of the Soviet Union in an ongoing Cold War to control the vast energy resources of the region - Uzbekistan, Azerbaijan, Kazakhstan and Turkmenistan - estimated to be worth $3 trillion.

The scene for these dramatic disclosures was an application for a Green Card in the Eastern District Court in Philadelphia by "controversial Islamic scholar" Fethullah Gulen who has been living in the United States since 1998. He argued that he was qualified for the Green Card as "an extraordinarily talented academic." The court case was covered extensively by the Turkish press.

Leading Turkish newspaper Hurriyet reported: "Gulen's financial resources were detailed in the public prosecutor's arguments, which claimed that Saudi Arabia, Iran, the Turkish government, and the Central Intelligence Agency, or CIA, were behind the Gulen movement. It stated that some businessmen in Ankara donated 10 to 70 percent of their annual income to the movement and that it corresponded to $20,000 to $300,000 per year per person. It added that one businessman in Istanbul donated $4-5 million each year and that young people graduating from Gulen's schools donated between $2,000 and $5,000 each year."

Among the reasons given by the US State attorneys as to why Gulen's permanent residence application was refused, is the suspicion of CIA financing of his movement. "There is even CIA suspicion because of the large amount of money that Gulen's movement uses to finance his projects, there are claims that he has secret agreements with Saudi Arabia, Iran, and Turkic governments. There are suspicions that the CIA is a co-payer in financing these projects," claimed the attorneys. Among the documents that the state attorneys presented, there are claims about the Gulen movement's financial structure and it was emphasized that the movement's economic power reached $25 billion. "Schools, newspapers, universities, unions, television channels . . . The relationship among these are being debated. There is no transparency in their work," claimed the attorneys.

Twenty six people wrote reference letters supporting Gulen's application for a Green Card - most notably ex-CIA agent George Fidas, former Turkish ambassador Morton Abramowitz, and former CIA Deputy Director Graham Fuller.

Those who believe the U.S. is behind Gulen typically make two arguments. First, they point to how Gulen got his green card in the first place. The long list of individuals who wrote letters of recommendations on Gulen's behalf includes two long-time CIA employees (George Fidas and Graham Fuller) and a former U.S. ambassador to Turkey (Morton Abramowitz). These individuals write in their individual capacities and their advocacy was based both on Gulen's persecution by the then-secularist Turkish judiciary and on Gulen's apparent promotion of a moderate brand of Islam.

On the latter question, at least, it is fair to assume that these recommenders had only limited knowledge of Gulen's full corpus, which includes some fairly incendiary stuff against Jews, Christians, the United States, and Western Europe.

However, the more important point about his green card -— and one that is overlooked in Turkey -- is that the U.S. administration was in fact opposed to giving Gulen a green card. It rejected Gulen's application, and then strenuously objected when Gulen's lawyers appealed. Lawyers for the Department of Homeland Security were scathing about Gulen's qualifications and argued there was no evidence he was an individual of exceptional ability in the field of education: "far from being an academic, plaintiff seeks to cloak himself with academic status by commissioning academics to write about him and paying for conferences at which his work is studied."

Gulen owes his residency not to the U.S. executive branch (and whichever intelligence agency may be hiding behind it), but to a federal judge with scant interest in foreign policy or intelligence matters who somehow nonetheless ruled in his favor. The judge's argument was that the Administration had construed the relevant field of "education" too narrowly, and should have considered Gulen's contributions to other areas such as "theology, political science, and Islamic studies."

Charter Schools

The second argument is that Gulen and his followers would not have been so successful in spreading their empire and influence without active U.S. support. I think this severely underestimates the movement's own capabilities. Gulen has long stressed education, organization, and secrecy. His movement has invested in raising a "golden generation" of smart, well-trained individuals. Lack of resources has never been a constraint, thanks to the contributions of an army of devout businessmen.

As the AKP found out to its own chagrin, its most capable and competent public servants turned out to be serving a different master in Pennsylvania. And in any case, this argument exaggerates U.S.' own capabilities: given the CIA's history of blunders, there is in fact much that it could learn from the Gulen movement on cloak-and-dagger operations.

The critical question here is whether there is anything the movement has done that it could not have done without active U.S. backing. Did it really need the help of some U.S. intelligence agency to expand its charter-school network, to stage the Sledgehammer trial, or to infiltrate and organize within the Turkish military?

The U.S. government may not have had a direct hand in Gulen's activities, but it is more difficult to dismiss the argument that it provided tacit support – or that some parts of the U.S. administration prevailed on other parts who were less keen on Gulen.

Judging by Wikileaks cables, U.S. diplomats in Turkey were exceptionally knowledgeable about Gulenist activities. These cables are in fact a goldmine of information on the Gulen movement. From these we learn, among others, about the elaborate ruses used by Gulenist sympathizers to infiltrate the Turkish army, Gulen's request for support from the Jewish Rabbinate's during his green card application, and the attempt by sympathizers within the Turkish national police to get a "clean bill of health" for Gulen from the U.S. consulate in Istanbul. We also learn that even in the heyday of their alliance, Gulenists presciently regarded Erdogan as a liability.

Perhaps of more direct interest to the U.S., foreign service officers have long been aware that many Turks have been obtaining visas under false pretenses, with the ultimate aim of ending up as teachers in Gulen's charter schools. Yet apparently nothing was ever done to stop this flow, nor to hold the movement to account. A ridiculous number of H-1B visas have been issued to Turkish teachers in these schools. One naturally wonders why the U.S. administration never clamped down on the Gulen movement for apparent visa fraud.

The same question arises with respect to the widespread pattern of financial improprieties that has been uncovered in Gulen's charter schools. A whistleblower has provided evidence that Turkish teachers are required to kick back a portion of their salary to the movement. The FBI has seized documents revealing preferential awarding of contracts to Turkish-connected businesses. Such improprieties are apparently still under investigation. But the slow pace at which the government has moved does make one suspect that there is no overwhelming desire to bring Gulen to justice.

Gulen typically defends himself against such charges by saying that the schools are run by sympathizers and are not directly under his control. Yet the fact is that he took direct credit for the schools in his green card application, saying he had overseen their establishment.

Sledgehammer case

Then there is the Sledgehammer case, which has the Gulen movement's fingerprints all over it. This and the closely related Ergenekon trials did untold damage to the military of U.S.' Nato ally. The jailing of hundreds of officers, including a former chief of staff, sowed a climate of fear and suspicion within the army and sapped military morale. Perhaps the U.S. was bamboozled, like many others, early on about these trials. But by now it should know that these sham trials were launched and stage managed by Gulenists. American officials have been quick to complain in public about the damage the post-coup purge has done to Turkish military capabilities. Yet there was not a peep from them during the Ergenekon and Sledgehammer witch hunts; and nor has the U.S. administration expressed any discontent about the Gulen movement's role in them since.

The failed coup

The mystery only deepens after the botched coup. The U.S. has demanded credible evidence from Turkey on Gulen's involvement, which is as it should be. But beyond that, it appears from the outside as if administration officials have been interested mostly in throwing cold water on the Turkish government's claim that Gulen was behind the coup – a claim that is largely justified.

The most egregious example is that of James Clapper, the Director of National Intelligence. Asked whether Turkish allegations that Gulen planned the attempted coup passed the "smell test" of credibility, Clapper answered: "No. Not to me." Clapper said Secretary of State Kerry "was right on the ball" to press the Turks to back up their extradition request with evidence of Gulen's involvement, adding: "We haven't seen it yet. We certainly haven't seen it in intel."

Now coming from the head of American intelligence, this is no less than a stunning statement. As the Wikileaks cables I referred to above make clear, the State Department, at least, has been well aware of Gulenist infiltration of the Turkish military for quite some time. The Gulenists's role in Sledgehammer, which led to the discharge of many of the most Kemalist/secularist officers in the military is equally clear. Beyond Sledgehammer, the Gulenists' wide range of clandestine operations against opponents in Turkey must be well known to American intelligence. So when the most senior intelligence officer in the U.S. instinctively brushes off Gulen's possible involvement, it looks awfully like he is either incompetent or has something to hide.

Since Clapper's statement was made, the head of the Turkish military, who was held hostage by the putschists during the coup attempt, has said that one of his captors offered to put him in touch with Gulen directly. This, on its own, is prima facie evidence of Gulen's involvement, and likely passes the "probable cause" test that is required for extradition. Incredibly, administration officials are still quoted as saying "there is no credible evidence of Mr. Gulen's personal involvement." In other words, these officials must think that the army chief of their NATO ally is lying.

In light of the confusing signals that come out of the U.S., and the apparent desire of many people in or close to the administration to defend Gulen, it's not difficult to empathize with those in Turkey who believe the U.S. must be behind Gulen (and, yes, even the coup attempt).

But it is not farfetched to think that there are some groups in the administration – perhaps in the intelligence branches – who have been protecting Gulen because they think he is useful to U.S. foreign policy interests. This could be because Gulen's brand/mask of moderate Islam is a rare thing in that part of the world. It could be because taking Gulen down would only benefit groups in Turkey they consider more inimical to U.S. interests – Erdogan's AKP and the arch-secularists.

It is even possible that the movement has occasionally performed services for U.S. intel operations. Some of Gulen's schools in Central Asia were used to "shelter" American spies according to a former Turkish intelligence chief. That kind of thing would not be beneath either the CIA or the Gulen movement.

Perhaps these groups have so far have had the better of the argument and have held the upper hand in the administration against those in State or elsewhere who know full well what the Gulen movement is up to and would rather see him go. In the aftermath of the coup, perhaps this balance will change in favor of the latter. Perhaps not. Whether it does or not, I think the Gulen issue will ultimately explode in somebody's face in the U.S. The only questions are whose, and when.

It is very unlikely that Gulen would receive a fair trial in Turkey. So the U.S. has a legitimate ground for not extraditing him. But the U.S. foreign policy establishment would be making a very big mistake if they simply dismissed the calls from Turkey about Gulen's complicity. It is easy for the U.S. to hide behind Erdogan's clampdown and the ill treatment of the putschists. But the U.S. has considerable explaining to do too.

Fuller

Graham E. Fuller had been immersed in the CIA's activities in steering Mujahideen and other political Islamic organizations since the 1980's. He spent 20 years as CIA operations officer in Turkey, Lebanon, Saudi Arabia, Yemen, and Afghanistan, and was one of the CIA's early advocates of using the Muslim Brotherhood and similar Islamist organizations like Gülen Cemaat to advance US foreign policy.

The Turkish media reports that none other than Gülen mentor, "former" CIA man Graham E. Fuller, along with another "former" CIA person and close Fuller associate, Henri J. Barkey, were at a luxury hotel on one of the Princes' Islands in the Sea of Marmara, some twenty minutes from Istanbul, on the night of July 15.

While Washington adamantly continues do deny any and all involvement in the failed July 15 Turkish coup attempt, Turkish media is revealing detailed information of the involvement of key US figures as alleged coup organizers. They include the former NATO International Security Assistance Force (Afghanistan) Commander, Army General John F. Campbell. And now new revelations name Henri J. Barkey, a former CIA man, now based as Bernard L. and Bertha F. Cohen Professor at Lehigh University in Bethlehem, Pennsylvania, conveniently, a mere 26 miles or 30 minute drive via PA-33 from Saylorsburg, home of the exiled Fethullah Gülen.

According to the Istanbul Yeni Safak paper, on the July 15 night of the coup Henri Barkey and a group of seventeen others, mostly foreigners, met for hours in a locked room in the Splendid Palas hotel on the tourist Princes' Island outside Istanbul and reportedly followed coup developments on TV amid their closed-door talks, according to testimony of hotel personnel. The paper cites a source from Istanbul Police's Intelligence, Counter Terror, Cyber Crime and Criminal Units, who reported that Barkey was holding a meeting at the hotel with 17 top figures, most of them foreign nationals, on July 15, the day of the failed coup attempt in Turkey.

According to the hotel management, Barkey had held a "meeting that lasted hours until the morning on July 16 in a special room. They have been following the coup attempt over TV channels," the hotel personnel told police.

Other reports from well-informed Turkish independent journalists say that among the members present with Barkey the night of the coup was former CIA senior officer and mentor of Fethullah Gülen, Graham E. Fuller, former CIA Station Chief in Turkey. Fuller and Barkey are both old Langley CIA associates. Both have long involvement with Turkish affairs. They even co-authored a book, Turkey's Kurdish Question.

Now Fuller again in his personal blog rushes to deny being behind Fethullah Gülen and the Turkish coup. His blog post is a rambling paean of praise for his protégé, Gülen, writing that "Gülen comes out of an apolitical, more Sufi, mystical and social tradition. Gülen is interested in slow, deep social change including secular higher education...looking at the dramatically failed coup attempt against Erdogan last week, I believe it is unlikely that Gülen was the mastermind behind it."

Despite Fuller's clumsy attempt to sheep-dip Gülen, it's been documented that the same CIA-backed Gülen organization, after the collapse of the Soviet Union in the 1990's, rushed to establish Gülen schools across former Soviet Central Asia republics from Turkey into Chechnya and Dagestan in Russia, into Uzbekistan, Kyrgyzstan and on into Xingiang, China.

In 1999, while at RAND, Fuller advocated using Muslim forces to further US interests in Central Asia against both China and Russia. He stated, "The policy of guiding the evolution of Islam and of helping them against our adversaries worked marvelously well in Afghanistan against the Russians. The same doctrines can still be used to destabilize what remains of Russian power, and especially to counter the Chinese influence in Central Asia."

Fuller's book, Turkey's New Geopolitics: From the Balkans to Western China, was published in 1993, just as Gülen's organization was establishing a string of Gülen schools targeting the local children of the elites in Central Asia all the way to Xinjiang Province in Western China, home of many Muslim Turkic Uyghurs. By the mid-1990s, more than seventy-five Gülen schools had spread to Kazakhstan, Tajikistan, Azerbaijan, Turkmenistan, Kyrgyzstan, Uzbekistan, and even to Dagestan and Tatarstan in Russia, amid the chaos of the post-Soviet Boris Yeltsin era.

In 2011, Osman Nuri Gündeş, former head of Foreign Intelligence for the Turkish MIT, the "Turkish CIA," and chief intelligence adviser in the mid-1990s to Prime Minister Tansu Çiller, published a bombshell book that was only released in Turkish. In the book, Gündeş, then 85 and retired, revealed that, during the 1990s, the Gülen schools then popping up across Central Asia were providing a base for hundreds of CIA agents under cover of being "native-speaking English teachers." According to Gündeş, the Gülen movement *sheltered 130 CIA agents*" at its schools in Kyrgyzstan and Uzbekistan alone.

The picture emerging of Gülen and his organization is hardly what Graham E. Fuller describes as "an a-political, more Sufi, mystical and social tradition." In fact Gülen was forced to flee to the USA at the end of the 1990's when Turkish secret police taped a closed-door sermon by Gülen to his closest followers in which he reportedly said, *"You must move in the arteries of the system without anyone noticing your existence until you reach all the power centers…You must wait for the time when you are complete and conditions are ripe, until we can shoulder the entire world and carry it…You must wait until such time as you have gotten all the state power…in Turkey…"*

Grahal Fuller wrote an article in Huffington Post a week after the coup: *"I believe it is unlikely that Gulen was the mastermind behind the dramatic failed coup attempt against Erdogan last week. Of course, in the absence of evidence, so far no one can speak with certainty. Gulen's social movement probably has well over a million followers or sympathizers who are not under centralized control.*

With the arrests of tens of thousands this week and the use of torture already suspected, there is no telling what kind of "confessions" will be generated. Erdogan demands that the U.S. extradite Gulen (he lives in Pennsylvania) to Turkey, but Washington does not usually extradite political figures unless the evidence is highly persuasive in a U.S. court.

Gulen has always embraced the importance and dignity of the state, in the best Ottoman tradition. He has supported the state against earlier Islamist movements that raised Islam over the state. He even felt compelled to support the military takeover of the state in 1980 in order to preserve the state in the face of raging guerrilla warfare raging in the streets. Basically, however, he supports democracy over military rule as the surest guarantee for the freedom of Hizmet to exist and conduct its social mission.

Furthermore, Hizmet does not engage in terrorist activities, so support for political violence in this case is extremely unlikely. Erdogan's charge that Hizmet is a "terrorist organization" is absurd to anyone with the least knowledge of the movement, given its strong emphasis on peace and dialogue.

But in the years of Bush's global war on terrorism, many neoconservatives in Washington were agitating to deport Gulen — among many hundreds of other Muslim clerics — as a security risk to the U.S. I found the charge baseless. Indeed, I still believe that Hizmet as a movement represents one of the most encouraging faces of contemporary Islam in the world.

I wanted the U.S. Federal Bureau of Investigation to at least be aware of my considered personal opinion as they considered his case. Since then, enemies of Gulen and many conspiratorial-minded Turks decided to connect the dots: the fact that I was a U.S. Central Intelligence Agency official (I had retired from the agency 18 years before) and that I had spoken out in defense of Gulen constituted clear "proof" that Gulen is a CIA agent.

That changed after Erdogan's Justice and Development Party (known as the AKP) came to power in 2002. Many members of Hizmet then became free to seek positions in government (if qualified). In particular, they sought jobs in the police and judiciary, to a large measure to ensure that police powers would never be wielded against them (or the AKP) again, as in the past. The tide has now turned, and the full powers of the Erdogan-controlled police are being used against Hizmet members. Sadly, the police have regularly been a political football in Turkish politics over the years

We are talking about a critical issue: what kind of movements will represent Islam's future? ISIS? Al Qaeda? The Muslim Brotherhood? As Islamic movements go, I would rank Hizmet high on the list of rational, moderate, socially constructive and open-minded organizations. It is not a cult; it sits squarely in mainstream modernizing Islam.

How will it end? Erdogan has beaten Hizmet decisively. But he is planting the seeds for his own destruction. How and when he will fall remains unclear. Meanwhile, on the international scene, Turkey is rapidly becoming a pariah. The country itself is now his primary victim..."

In the interest of full disclosure — it is on public record that I wrote a letter as a private citizen in connection with Gulen's U.S. green card application in 2006, stating that I did not believe that Gulen constituted a security threat to the U.S. This came shortly after I had finished a book, The Future of Political Islam, that involved extensive travel and interviews with Islamists around the world. In that context, I found Hizmet to be remarkably moderate, tolerant, non-violent, open to dialogue, a social rather than political movement, and a strong proponent of education as the means to empower Muslims in a globalizing future.

This is my attempt at providing a reasoned answer to the question. My conclusion in brief: I don't think Gulen is a tool of the U.S. or has received support from the U.S. for its clandestine operations. But it is possible that some elements within the U.S. national security apparatus think Gulen furthers their agenda, is worth protecting on U.S. soil, and have so far prevailed on other voices in the establishment with different views. Regardless, the U.S. needs to seriously reconsider its attitude towards Gulen and his movement.

All evidence suggests that NATO Turkish Gladio networks picked up Gülen as a potentially useful asset years ago. As their agenda changed with the collapse of the Soviet Union, their role for Gülen changed as well and doors were opened for him to play that role.

So in a true sense we can say that the Gülen Cemaat is the nothing more than the projection of an idea from Langley Virginia CIA headquarters, an idea from people there who believed they could use him and they could abuse religion as a cover to advance their design for global control, what David Rockefeller calls One World Government.

Unlike the CIA's Mujahideen Jihadists like Hekmatyar in Afghanistan or Naser Oric in Bosnia, the CIA decided to give Fethullah Gülen a radically different image. No blood-curdling, head-severing, human-heart-eating Jihadist. Fethullah Gülen was presented to the world as a man of "peace, love and brotherhood," even managing to grab a photo Op with Pope John Paul II, which Gülen featured prominently on his website. The Gülen organization in the US hired one of Washington's highest-paid Public Relations image experts, George W. Bush's former campaign director, Karen Hughes, to massage his "moderate" Islam image.

Banned in Russia

Russian intelligence agency, the FSB, has repeatedly taken action against the Gulen movement for acting as a front organization for the CIA. In December 2002, Turkish newspaper Hurriyet reported: "Russian secret service claims: Turkish religious brotherhood works for CIA... The FSB, the Russian intelligence organization formerly called the KGB, has claimed that the 'Nurcus' religious brotherhood in Turkey has engaged in espionage on behalf of the CIA through the companies and foundations it has founded."

FSB head Nikolay Patrushev has mentioned the names of these companies and foundations, saying, 'The brotherhood engages in anti-Russian activities via two companies, Serhad and Eflak, as well as foundations such as Toros, Tolerans and Ufuk.' Patrushev has accused the brotherhood of conducting pan-Turkish propaganda, of trying to convert Russian youths to Islam by sowing the seeds of enmity, and of engaging in certain lobbying activities. These companies and foundations have turned up in the internet site of Fethullah Gulen"... Russia has banned all of Gulen's madrassas, and in April of this year, banned the Nurcu Movement completely.

The Gulen Movement founded madrassas all over the world in the 1990's, most of them in the newly independent Turkic republics of Central Asia - Azerbaijan, Turkmenistan, Uzbekistan, Kazakhstan and Kyrgyzstan - and Russia. These madrassas appear to be used as a front for enabling CIA and State Department officials to operate undercover in the region, with many of the teachers operating under diplomatic passports.

Gulen Schools in USA

After the fall of the Soviet Union, Gulen's followers established hundreds of schools in the newly independent Central Asian countries, attempting to rekindle a Turkish cultural kinship there. Around the world, there are more than a dozen universities affiliated with the Gulen Movement, including three in the U.S.

Virginia International University is located in Fairfax, Virginia, American Islamic College in Chicago, Illinois, and North American University in Houston, Texas. None displays any hint of a Gulen Movement connection at its website, but the American Islamic College's Board of Trustees alone should set alarm bells ringing.

Among the listed Board members is one Dr. Abdullah Omar Naseef, a Saudi closely-connected not only to the royal family but to both al-Qa'eda and the Muslim Brotherhood as well. He was, in fact, a top al-Qa'eda financier prior to 9/11 as founder of the Rabita Trust, a formally designated foreign terrorist organization under American law.

Naseef also founded the Institute of Muslim Minority Affairs and served on its journal's editorial board for a period of at least seven years (1996-2003) together with Huma Abedin, who was working through the period at the White House and elsewhere in various capacities for Hillary Clinton.

The Gulen Movement also is closely affiliated with the University of Houston, where the Gulen Institute, which bills itself as a 'non-profit research organization dedicated to the `promotion of peace and civic welfare,' is a joint initiative of the Graduate College of Social Work and the Institute of Interfaith Dialogue. According to its website, the Gulen Institute 'offers research grants and scholarships, organizes lecture series at the University of Houston, and facilitates workshops and panel discussions…' and also offers 'cultural exchange trips to graduate students at the University of Houston…'

Gulen K-12 charter schools

Gulen K-12 charter schools draw the most attention and concern. Since the first Gulen school in the U.S. opened in 1999, the network as grown to some 150 Gulenist schools with over 60,000 students enrolled in the U.S. Board members of these charter schools are primarily Turkish or Turkic (as are the overwhelmingly foreign-born male teachers and school administrators) and often have ties to other Gulenist organizations.

GM schools are funded in part by private donations from the far-flung movement's supporters but, as charters in the U.S., are also taxpayer-subsidized. Gulen schools typically emphasize a strong STEM (Science, Technology, Engineering, and Math) curriculum, which usually yields high test scores and students who excel academically. This is the part parents tend to love, but it's the more subtle messaging that increasingly is giving rise to concern. There is no evidence that Gulen charter schools in the U.S. include Islamic indoctrination in their curriculum, and yet, as the account below reveals, there clearly is at a minimum, a pro-Turkish agenda that infuses the program.

For instance, GM charter schools usually include Turkish language classes, which may be mandatory in some grade levels, an overt emphasis on Turkish culture, and student participation in Turkish Language Olympics. The GM schools' Turkish agenda was inadvertently exposed when a 2009 GM Turkish-language website ('Sabah') revealed a disturbing conversation among the writer, Nazli Ilicak, and other GM colleagues.

"We discussed the subject among ourselves: If 600 schools are bought this way in the United States — and that's what the members of the

Gulen movement are striving to do, - and if 200 students graduate from each one of these schools, then 120 thousand sympathizers of Turkey join the mainstream out there every year. We are trying to lobby against the Armenian genocide resolution every year. And yet, through education, we can teach tens of thousands of people the Turkish language and our national anthem, introduce them to our culture and WIN them over. And this is what the Gulen movement is striving for."

Once the GM realized the conversation had been translated into English and made public in the U.S., it disappeared from the original website. Likewise, when GM school officials are questioned about their school's connections to the GM, the responses are often either ambiguous or flat denials. The argument filed with the Department of Homeland Security (DHS) on Gulen's behalf when he was appealing a DHS ruling that he did not meet the criteria to qualify as an "alien of extraordinary ability" for purposes of immigration to the U.S., however, offers the most compelling evidence of precisely such connections.

According to the Philadelphia Inquirer, Gulen's successful appeal, that won him a green card from a federal judge in 2008, emphasized his renown as an educational figure. The Washington Post went even further, writing that Gulen's lawyers had openly "identified him as 'head of the Gulen Movement,' and an important educational figure who had 'overseen' the creation of a network of schools in the U.S. and around the world."

All of which apparently deliberate ambiguity contributes to the network's secretive image and growing concern among educators, law enforcement, and parents that such schools may function to some extent as a feeder system to the GM itself. Even a devote as sympathetic to Fethullah Gulen as Hakan Yavuz, assistant professor at the University of Utah's Middle East Center, and the co-author (together with Georgetown's John Esposito) of a laudatory book on the GM, "Turkish Islam and the Secular State: the Gulen Movement," was honest enough to tell the New York Times the truth about the GM's Islamic agenda.

According to the Times, Yavuz said that he sees the [Gulen] schools as *"the foundation for the movement's attempts to grow in the United States. The main purpose right now is to show the positive side of Islam and to make Americans sympathize with Islam."*

The extent to which the multi-faceted GM is organized within the U.S. similarly is not well-understood, but reporting that has emerged suggests a far more structured administrative apparatus than generally realized. For example, in 2012, a Turkish teacher who formerly taught at a U.S. Gulen school told the FBI that the Movement *'had divided the U.S. into five regions, with a general manager in each who coordinates the activities of the schools, and related foundations and cultural centers.'*

Additionally, Gulen charter schools regularly sponsor trips to Turkey for students. GM-associated organizations, not all of which openly identify themselves as connected to the Gulen Movement, but rather present as Turkish 'cultural' groups, have also provided thousands of all-expenses-paid trips to Turkey for academics, journalists, politicians and other public officials. Sightseeing is a big part of such 'cultural immersion' trips, but so are visits to GM-affiliated institutions.

Although GM leadership denies that there is any top-down organized attempt to seek political influence through donations to political campaigns in the U.S. or the hundreds of all-expense-paid trips to Turkey that have been provided to key members of local, state, and federal legislatures, evidence of such involvement has been mounting. For example, campaign donations from people connected to Gulen schools to Texas Congressional Representative Sheila Jackson Lee totaled $23,000 in October 2013, which was a considerable sum, given that, according to documents filed with the Federal Election Commission, she raised a total of $130,000 that particular election cycle.

Other liberal Democrats, including Yvette Clarke and Al Green, and conservative Republicans like Ted Poe and Pete Olson, have all benefitted from donors affiliated with Gülen in one way or another.

In response, GM representatives point out that the Movement is a nonprofit, non-governmental organization that does not endorse candidates or engage in political fundraising for any candidates. Concerns about the GM, including a look at its U.S. network of charter schools, were aired on a 60 Minutes piece with reporter Leslie Stahl in May 2012.

A GM watchdog group, has compiled a long list of accounts about trips to Turkey sponsored and paid for by a host of various Gulen affiliates, including the Atlas Foundation of Louisiana, the Raindrop Foundation, several different U.S. branches of the Dialogue Foundation, the Niagara Foundation, the North Carolina-based Divan Center, the Pacifica Institute, and others.

Those targeted for such junkets included civic leaders, Christian and Jewish faith community leaders, journalists, state legislators, students, and university presidents, professors, and trustees. Typically, according to recorded trip accounts, those invited know that it is the GM that sponsors them, but seem often to be carefully selected for their lack of familiarity about Fethullah Gulen or his agenda related to Islam and Turkey.

The Gulenists do not always reveal their sponsorship of all-expense-paid trips to Turkey, however. In the case of hundreds of trips for members of the U.S. Congress, GM funding was in fact carefully concealed. A USA Today investigation reported on 29 October 2015 that the GM secretly and illegally funded "as many as 200 trips to Turkey" for members of Congress since 2008.

According to investigators, the House Ethics Committee approved all of the trips based on allegedly falsified disclosure forms that disguised the Gulenist identities of groups that presented themselves as non-profit organizations.

The FBI and the Department of Labor and Education have begun investigating at least two practices of concern involving the Gulen schools nationwide: their extraordinarily high and disproportionate utilization of H-1B visas to import teachers and other personnel from Turkey to staff their charter schools, and the reportedly higher pay for Turkish staffers who are then compelled to return a portion of their salaries to Hizmet (that is, to the Gulen Movement).

Foreign-trained teachers and other workers are eligible for employment in the U.S. via the H-1B non- immigrant work visa which is good for 3 years, renewable for one additional 3 year term, or the shorter 1 year J-1 exchange visa, which is renewable for an additional 2 year term. The J-1 visa is intended to promote cultural exchange. The H-1B visa allows hiring foreign workers in a "specialty occupation that requires theoretical and practical application of a body of highly specialized knowledge, along with at least a bachelor's degree or its equivalent in the specialization".

Even though there is an annual cap on the number of H-1B visas that can be issued, primary and secondary schools in some instances can circumvent the cap. Federal law has exempted institutions of higher education, nonprofit and government research institutions, and institutions related to or affiliated with them, from the visa cap. For example, a Texas school district was able to access this exemption by having its bilingual teachers hired through a university certification program, which included a 2 month public school internship.

The typical claim made by school districts and/or charter schools utilizing the H-1B visas for foreign recruitment of teachers and other school personnel, is the "shortage" of qualified American workers. But "the H-1B program demands no test of the labor market by employers (to see if American workers are available for these jobs)..." and as Center for Immigration Studies fellow David North notes, operates to "deprive American teachers of jobs".

Abundant documentation and first-hand testimony exist to support the allegations that the Gulen-affiliated network of schools is the largest consumer of H-1B visas for school staffing in the U.S. Indeed, it has been reported that these schools exceed the application rate for these visas of even the largest urban school districts.

The Gulen schools and their related organizations account for 31.5% of all H-1B visa applications requested by the top 100 secondary school education H1B visa sponsors. Of the top 100 secondary school education H-1B visa sponsors, of the 100 sponsors were Gulen schools or their related organizations. A total of 4,277 secondary school visas were requested by the top 100 sponsors and of these, Gulen schools, or their related organizations, submitted 1,349

Specific charter school ties to Gülen can also be established. Cosmos Foundation operates charter schools in Texas under the name Harmony Science Academy. They also have ties to established charter schools in Oklahoma and Louisiana and are petitioning the opening of a school in New Mexico.

State funded schools

This is a potential issue for these charter schools. The schools are funded by federal and state tax revenues. At the federal level, this means there is potential conflict with the Establishment Clause of the First Amendment of the U.S. Constitution which implies tax dollars are not allowed to fund religious institutions. The state level is where the schools could potentially have their biggest legal troubles. Most of the states' charter school legislation has language similar to that of the State of Pennsylvania which reads, "a charter school shall benon-sectarian in all operations." Some 'outsiders' have taken notice of the movement's increased activity concluding, "Gülenism is essencially a cult." and is a "cult of sorts." Coupling this all together, It is clear why these schools do not want to be labeled Gülen schools.

Many parents seem happy with the education their students are receiving. Partly due to the school's success and more to do with the fervor of the Fethullahci, there has been a tremendous surge in the opening of these schools over the past five years. This momentum does not seem to be slowing, even with numerous states cutting education budgets due to poor economic conditions.

With rapid growth and increased, nationwide visibility, it is inevitable that more scrutiny and questions will be raised as to the nature of these schools. It will be interesting to watch how the Movement and the schools respond to this attention in the future.

FBI investigation

In October 2015, USA Today gave front-page, above-the-fold treatment to such Gulenist influence operations, revealing that federal investigators had determined that Gulen Movement fronts paid for hundreds of trips to Turkey for members of the U.S. Congress and their staff while illegally concealing the actual source of that funding. In addition, the FBI and other federal agencies are investigating numerous other allegations of irregularities at GM charter schools across the country.

While much has been published about Gulen and his movement, the most revealing passages ultimately come not from investigative reporters or critics, but from Fethullah Gulen himself in a book he wrote in 1998: Prophet Mohammed as Commander.

A concluding segment of this monograph quotes extensively from that work, because it is so revealing of Gulen's thinking about how jihad should be practiced against the "unbelievers" or infidels in countries like ours. The following passage is as illustrative as it should be alarming:

"...[Muslim] believers should also equip themselves with the most sophisticated weaponry. Force has an important place in obtaining the desired result, so believers cannot be indifferent to it. Rather they must be much more advanced in science and technology than unbelievers so that they should not allow unbelievers to use "force" for their selfish benefit. According to Islam, "right is might"; so, in order to prevent might from being right in the hands of unbelievers and oppressors, believers must be mightier than others.

An Islamic state...should be able to secure peace and justice in the world and no power should have the courage to make corruption in any part of the earth. This will be possible when Muslims equip themselves with a strong belief and righteousness in all their affairs, and also with scientific knowledge and the most sophisticated technology.

Mossad

The failed coup in Turkey and subsequent events are having a strong effect on Israeli-Turkish relations, namely they have put a complete freeze on the reconciliation process between the two countries. The Turkish government is now focused on tightening its grip on society by persecuting and purging the military, intelligence and practically all other security and civilian structures of the state from its real or imaginary enemies.

After Mavi Marmara

More than six years after the relations between the two countries deteriorated as a result of the tragic incidents of the Mavi Marmara, representatives of the two governments signed a reconciliation agreement at the end of June 2016 in a Rome hotel.

The Mavi Marmara was a Turkish boat which carried Turkish and international "peace" activists who wanted to break the Israeli siege and reach Gaza. The ship was purchased in 2010 by IHH, a Turkish NGO active as a charity organization in more than 115 countries.

But Israeli intelligence sources claimed that IHH smuggled weapons on behalf of terrorist groups and had links to al-Qaeda. In 2010, the US State Department expressed great concern over the group's links with senior Hamas officials.

In May 2010, while sailing on international waters enroute to Gaza, the boat was stopped by the Israeli navy. For Israel, most of the passengers were terrorists or at least agents of provocation who were equipped with clubs, chains, and bats and came to cause trouble, not humanitarians. The clashes resulted in the death of nine Turkish citizens and the humiliation of one of Israel's top commando units – Flotilla 13.

Turkish needs

The reconciliation agreement contains diplomatic, economic and security-related topics. The most annoying clause from the Israeli side is the readiness is to pay $20m to the Turkish families of the victims.

Just for the perspective, Israel reluctantly paid relatively less to the victims' families of the USS Liberty, a spy ship of the US's National Security Agency which sailed near the Sinai Peninsula coastline during the 1967 war. The Israeli Air Force mistook the Liberty for an enemy ship, attacked it and killed 34 crewmen.

However, Turkey needed the agreement much more than Israel did. Erdogan's foreign and security policies have failed completely since the bloody civil war in Syria began more than five years ago. He announced that his policy would revolve around "zero" troubles with his neighbours. Exactly the opposite has characterised it: Turkey has found itself in disputes with the Basher Assad regime in Syria and with Russia, Iran, the Islamic State and Kurds at home and in Syria.

Israeli demands

Thus, the new deal contains some positive elements and advantages for Israel. Turkey bent to Israeli pressure and agreed to shut down an office established by Izz A-Din Qassam, the military wing of Hamas. From this office in Istanbul, as Israeli intelligence officials would later disclose in a briefing, Hamas operatives had issued orders, sent money and ran terror operatives in the occupied West Bank against Israel and the Palestinian Authority (PA).

In 2015, the Israel Security Agency (ISA also known as Shin Bet) foiled a few attempts of these kinds, the largest almost a year ago, when dozens of Hamas members were arrested and caches of weapons found.

The orders were given personally by Salah al-Aruri, the Turkey-based Hamas commander who benefited from the personal protection of Hakan Fidan, the chief of Turkey's National Intelligence Organisation (MIT). To the agony of Fidan, Erdogan gave orders to expel Aruri already a few months ago. Fidan doesn't like Israel. Over the past six years, he tried to avoid meeting his Mossad counterparts. He seldom met Tamir Pardo, the former director of Mossad, and his successor, Yossi Cohen, and reduced the links between the two agencies to the minimum.

Mossad suspected that Fidan was pro-Iranian and American intelligence sources accused him of informing Iran about an Israeli espionage ring operating on Iranian soil. As a result, Iranian citizens were arrested.

Historic intelligence ties

The special security and intelligence ties between the two countries began in the second half of the 1950s. Encourage by the US and the UK, the intelligence communities of Israel (Mossad), Iran (Savak) and Turkey (MIT) established a tripartite consultative body known as the Trident alliance.

The intelligence chiefs of the three services met annually and exchanged information on common enemies – Egypt, Syria and Iraq. The relations reached their peak in the 1950s, with Iran's involvement ending after the country's 1979 revolution. Israeli-Turkish intelligence sharing continued through the first decade of the 21st century, peaking in the mid-2000s and ending when Erdogan walked away.

Turkey became an important market worth several billion dollars for Israeli military and security goods. Israeli security corporations sold drones, intelligence equipment and upgraded fighter planes and tanks for the Turkish army.

Turkey also fed Israel with information which it had obtained about Syria, Iraq and, to certain degree, Iran from its spies and listening posts built by the US. In return, Turkey asked for and got information obtained by Israeli intelligence on Kurdish organisations especially the PKK.

Mossad officials met regularly with their MIT colleagues either in Ankara or Istanbul or in Tel Aviv. During some of these sessions, senior MIT officials in charge of monitoring the PKK even felt at ease and close enough to ask their Israeli counterparts if they would be willing to help them to assassinate Kurdish terrorists. The Israelis listened politely, usually didn't comment and ignored the requests.

It all ended when then Turkish prime minister, now president, Erdogan changed the course of Turkish foreign policy and orientation.

It is clear to Israeli security officials that when the new agreement is implemented, the golden era of close, even intimate military and intelligence cooperation between Israel and Turkey, will not return.

The great irony in the coup attempt that failed in Turkey was obvious. President Recep Tayyip Erdogan has tried for years to stifle the operating freedom of social networks and has accused them of being dark forces attempting to undermine his rule. It was these same social media networks which helped him to put down the coup.

Erdogan broadcast from his smartphone — using Apple's FaceTime — a statement to the people. He tweeted to his supporters and relied on the media, even those whom he deathly hates, to spread his message in the critical first hours of the coup attempt when uncertainty gripped the country.

In the case of Turkey, it seems that those involved – apparently relatively low-ranked officers – would not have succeeded in their operation even if Erdogan would not have been able to deliver his broadcast.

The rebellion initially appeared to be going by the book. The rebels gained control of the bridges over the Bosphorous Strait in Istanbul, which connect Europe and Asia, as well as major junctions. Pilots involved in the plot bombed the parliament building in Ankara, the MIT intelligence agency's headquarters and some military strongpoints, including tanks near the presidential palace.

They even took control of the state-run TV station, TRT, and forced a remarkably poised female newscaster to read their statement that they had taken over the government to preserve democracy, to remove Erdogan, to suppress terrorism, and to change the Constitution.

However, it appears that the number of soldiers in their command – apparently a few thousand – was insufficient to complete the job.

In Turkey's previous four military coups since 1960, tens of thousands of soldiers took part, if not the entire army. This time, the rebels kidnapped the chief of staff and a number of other senior commanders, who have since been freed, but most importantly they failed to capture Erdogan, who was vacationing at a Marble Lake resort. Capturing the Turkish leader was probably the first thing they should have done.

Erdogan succeeded in broadcasting his remarks to the people, calling on his supporters to take to the streets, and they answered his call. They blocked the rebel soldiers' path and together with the police, which remained loyal to Erdogan, fought them and took many of them prisoner.

Anytime that the military commanders believed that the civilian leadership was straying from the constitution, they did not hesitate to carry out a coup, take rule into their own hands and eventually put a democratic government back in place.

For years now, there has been disillusionment within the army and the secular public with Erdogan, the leader of the Islamist AKP party. As prime minister and elected president he instituted a dictatorship in the hopes of establishing himself as a 21st century sultan, while increasing the influence of religion in the public sphere. This is also the reason that Erdogan purified institutions in the state and instituted changes within them to strengthen his hold on power.

He put his loyalists in key positions in Turkey's intelligence agency, police, justice system, education system and the army. He harassed the media, trying to take it over and marginalized business leaders who he saw as hostile to the throne.

It can be assumed that now, with the defeat of the coup attempt, he will immediately increase his efforts to strengthen his hold on power and oppress his opponents. His supporters are already accusing his arch rival Fethullah Gulen, a powerful cleric who lives in exile in the U.S., of organizing the rebellion. Gulen has denied involvement, but that will not stop Erdogan from persecuting Gulen's supporters.

Despite the fact that the U.S. and most members of NATO, to which Turkey belongs, condemned the coup and voiced support for Erdogan and the elected government, there is no doubt that there is increasing concern among them about instability in the country.

As for Israel, which just recently signed a reconciliation deal with Turkey, the failure of the coup will not affect relations between the countries and the status quo will continue. However, it can be assumed that the Israeli government, the defense establishment and the intelligence community would not have shed a tear if the coup had succeeded, Erdogan had been ousted and the army had taken power.

Even if Israel and Turkey soon announce an end to their diplomatic crisis, which began almost six years ago as a result of the Mavi Marmara flotilla ship incident, relations between the two countries will not go back to how they once were.The golden era of cooperation in the security and intelligence fields between the two countries up until a decade ago will certainly not come back.

Turkey is now more isolated than ever and is therefore interested in renewing ties with Israel, in the hope that the Jewish state can help Ankara improve its standing in Washington. Turkey also needs natural gas from Israel in order to diversify its sources of energy and to reduce its dependency on Russian gas.

Most of the disagreements between Israel and Turkey stemming from the Marmara incident have already been rectified. Prime Minister Benjamin Netanyahu apologized for the incident in which nine Turkish citizens were killed. Israel has already made clear that it is prepared to pay some $25 million in compensation to the families of the victims.

Turkey has deported senior Hamas military wing official Salah Aruri from the country and has tightened its supervision of the organization's members at Israel's request. Ankara has also agreed to institute special legislation that will prevent IDF commanders from standing trial for the Marmara incident.

Coming years

The key factors that can facilitate purge of the Gulenists are closely connected to the organizational structure of the network. There is a hierarchically organized network and the leader of the organization, Fethullah Gülen, has himself absolute command and direct control over the entire organization. It is very difficult to manage such a complicated organization with operations in almost 140 countries and those who are placed in the middle ranks of the organization are only chains in its command and control system.

In the short term the main challenges, in order to deal with Gulenists, are to dissolve the organizational structure, cut the material and human sources of the organization and to purge the militants and supporters from bureaucracy and civil society. The medium term challenge is the problem of radicalization of the militants and followers. When they are removed from the bureaucracy they may be immediately radicalized and resort to violence to destabilize Turkey. They may create crime networks, mafia style organizations and other secret illegal networks to threaten ordinary people and officials.

Therefore, in the long term the main challenge is to de-radicalize the body of the followers. This will be a long term challenge but the religious scholars, social scientists and bureaucrats need to deal with the "Gülenist belief system", delegitimize the deviant symbolic system, replacing it with legitimate conventional beliefs.

The struggle against the Gulenists will be a long and a challenging process, which needs to be well coordinated and the entire Turkish society should own this struggle like a national struggle. The aspect of public diplomacy is also another essential dimension. The most challenging aspect of this struggle is the international one.

Sleeping cells and hiding militants will most likely continue but if they are not connected to their leader or their superiors they can hardly function. Therefore, decapitation and containment of the leadership and the elite structure of the organization is crucial. Because of their messianic and apocalyptic views they may not consider the great purge within the bureaucracy as the ultimate defeat of the organization, they will rather continue to believe that when the time is right they will resurrect and take the control of Turkey and probably the entire world.

The loyalists of the organization believe that they are on the right side of the history and those of who try to contain them are destined to fail. It is very difficult to convince them about anything else. Using the Islamic texts and some other sources, Gülen has formulated a messianic narrative, which is quite difficult to defeat.

It must also be kept in mind that many of the loyalists of Gulen join the organization in the beginning because of their quest for a better education, position within the bureaucracy, faster promotion to the higher ranks of bureaucracy and for a business network. The Gulenists network has provided many opportunities to its members and loyalists. Looking at Turkish society as a whole, more effort must be made for equal opportunities to be provided to people in education, the bureaucracy and business so that they are not be vulnerable to this kind of clandestine body.

In order to eliminate domestic establishment of the organization, this aforementioned hierarchy can be purged by deciphering its institutions and actors. Due to its hierarchical characteristic, the organization might be dissolved when the leader, who keeps the organization together, is decapitated. When hierarchy fails, it is not possible for such organizations to ensure their existence unlike other secret organizations that are set-up in a cell system. However, credence to system does not decline as long as the leader is still in power because members of such organizations are absolutely committed to their leader.

The main momentum that leads to elimination of the organization is to overthrow Gülen, the leader of the organization. Elimination of the leader would be very decisive for the struggle because Gülen's spiritual leader ship and influence over his organization is the main impetus for the members to ensure its survival. For this reason, Turkey should request the deportation of Gülen and also should ensure the rehabilitation and normalization of Gülenist youth.

Gulenists are already organized in the judiciary, police department, education system, bureaucracy, military, business, and academic circles. The fact that Gulen's known affiliations in the military have been eliminated does not mean that the organization is totally wiped out. National security risks will remain particularly in sectors that the organization is still active and well-organized.

In short term, total elimination of the organization is not easy. In long term, the organization will remain in the establishment by effacing itself through mingling with other groups. By doing so, the organization with its messianic understanding will be biding the next reorganization moment. The main danger in this process is that the organization attempts to smuggle itself into other civilian organizations, NGOs, and networks.

The fight against this organization will take many years, however, it will not be possible for the struggle to be maintained consistently if governments and actors who operate against the organization change. Thus, a well-planned, gradual but urgent struggle is essential. It also should be kept in mind that if this purging process is delayed and diffused, the possibility of militants and sympathizer to hide themselves increases. It is therefore crucial to act rapidly and in a very coordinated manner until the visible elements of the organization are completely wiped out.

Some secret layers and segments of the organization will never be completely wiped out in the next couple of decades. Therefore an official institution composed of police, intelligence officials, judges and academics which is especially expert in fighting against this organization is an absolute necessity.

In particular, governmental and bureaucratic actors should establish strategic communication units in order to manage the complications, which are derived from the fact that crucial and top secret governmental information is in wrong hands. A new judicial framework is also required in order to ensure that the relevant actors can take actions.

Gulenists are particularly well-organized in civil society and the Turkish education system. In short term, it is not easy to eliminate the social capital that Gulenists have obtained by developing warm relations with the public. Sanitizing all institutions will spread over time since the organization is well-organized in business, education system, judicial system, and the medical sector. The organization will strive to find new ways and methods in order to maintain its existence, thus it will try ensure its association if not its activities. The government has to follow up structures that the organization has hidden itself in. The domestic dimension of the struggle will be tough and comprehensive.

Due to their capability to cover themselves within other groups, it might not be easy for Turkish officials to totally eliminate the organization. The fact that the members of the organization who are in the military and police have guns and they are expert in the use of sophisticated weaponry is a significant risk. The government should locate these weapons and prevent third-parties from seizing them.

At this moment nobody knows whether this organization has hidden weapons from the military in secret places to start a guerrilla style uprising against the government. The members of the organization might drag Turkey into an unstable process by using these guns. These weapons must be found and registered to official institutions.

The next and the hardest task is to struggle with their international network and institutions. Some states and intelligence agencies might use them in order to weaken and threaten Turkey and Gulenists can threat Turkey's interests by aligning with other states. Turkey needs to persuade other states in order to struggle with them in the domestic realm. Presenting materials that can assist judicial process is not adequate for persuading other states.

Assassinations

In the following period, the biggest threat that might come from the isolated, radicalized and illegitimate organization is political and civilian assassinations. Further, the organization can also trigger the civil war dynamics of Turkey by provoking the public. The only way to deal with these potential threats is to restore and strengthen the social peace. The assassination squads of Gulenists may conceal themselves in various institutions including other terrorist groups such as the PKK and the DHKPC.

www.ingramcontent.com/pod-product-compliance
Lightning Source LLC
Chambersburg PA
CBHW051948280526

45789CB00009B/3210